EVERYDAY
PALMISTRY

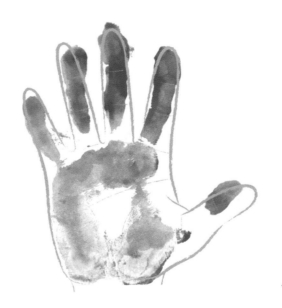

EVERYDAY
PALMISTRY

The key to character is in your hands

Heather Roan Robbins

CICO BOOKS

LONDON NEW YORK

This book is dedicated to the memory of Annie Laurie Walker Hemsworth,
the grandmother who still guides me through my dreams.

Published in 2016 by CICO Books
An imprint of Ryland Peters & Small Ltd
20–21 Jockey's Fields   341 E 116th St
London WC1R 4BW   New York, NY 10029

www.rylandpeters.com

10 9 8 7 6 5 4 3 2 1

A CIP catalog record for this book is available from the
Library of Congress and the British Library.

ISBN: 978-1-78249-373-0

Printed in China

Editor: Marion Paull
Design concept: Louise Leffler
Designer: Geoff Borin
Illustrator: Stephen Dew

Commissioning editor: Kristine Pidkameny
Senior editor: Carmel Edmonds
Art director: Sally Powell
Head of production: Patricia Harrington
Publishing manager: Penny Craig
Publisher: Cindy Richards

PICTURE CREDITS

CONTENTS

INTRODUCTION

An easy philosophy of palmistry

My funny, wise high-school art history teacher, Sushil Mukherjee, was also a wonderful tabla player and palmist. One day he pulled me aside and asked me to take special care of Coal, a friend nicknamed for her glowing spirit, because she had a nearly invisible life line, among many other worrisome signs. "Just keep an eye on her," he said. I was curious. I had already been studying astrology for several years but now I became obsessed about the hand, and pumped him for all the information I could get. He showed me the lay of the hand and taught me how to use the details to peer into this window of the soul.

Once the word got out, friends started giving me any book on palmistry they found as long as I looked at their hands in return, and my library built up quickly. I collected Xerox copies of hands and old-school palm prints made with an ink roller and wood block ink. I took many prints of my contemporaries' hands, young people whose lives and hands were still so malleable, and watched the patterns on their hands change in response to their choices to pick up or give up drugs or to apply their mind to study. In more dramatic cases, I saw their lines strengthen when they walked away from abusive families or gave up thoughts of suicide and chose to live. The lines in our hands change much faster when we are young and still forming the path of our life's journey, but we can see these changes at any age when we turn a major corner or make an effort to improve our condition.

Coal had many habits that prioritized living intensely (a wiry head and heart line) but not safety or health (faint, barely visible life line with many blocking lines, small mount of the Sun). A few years later she was murdered while hitchhiking alone, manifesting the concerns Sushil saw in her hand, but everybody else had missed.

I came to realize that Coal had a great map for healing in her hand. If she wanted to create more balance, she could use this map to prioritize self-care and probably live a longer time. But palmistry also gave me a map to accept my friend and her choices. Although I missed her dearly, I realized that if Coal truly felt she had only a little energy

to spend in this life, she chose to live it with gusto. Since then, I have seen people with faint life lines make healthier choices, grow stronger and more vital, and live a nice long time.

After seeing this evidence of palmistry's validity, I read everything on it I could get my hands on. I found that the early source material, from the late 1800s and early 1900s, had invaluable information from early massive surveys of hands. Both Cheiro (Irish astrologer William Warner) and William G. Benham gave us original theories and some great case histories, but neither had distilled their systems down to an accessible pattern. Several Middle Eastern and Asian books contained great information not found in the West, but you often had to read through sexist misconceptions, such as "in a man's hand this brings great scientific insight, in a woman's it makes a good housekeeper."

A line of palmistry books came out in the 1980s and 1990s, incorporating a new, humanistic, psychological awareness. A few of them, such as Judith Hipskind's *Palmistry: The Whole View*, were fresh, clear, and focused, but too many of them just imposed an undigested form of pop psychology combined with personal projection on traditional palmistry.

While my children were young, I took a day job in the human-resources field, worked psychic fairs across New England, and grew my private practice, and this gave me ample opportunity to test out all my theories. I watched the hands of people I met in business, at the store, in schools. I tossed out parts of traditional palmistry that just didn't seem to hold up, and distilled what worked, so I could teach palmistry through understanding rather than memorization.

A few articles were written about my work in palmistry in the 1980s and 1990s, but as I traveled, I found that astrology was an easier tool to use with distant clients than palmistry, although I'm always excited when clients send in photographs of their hands. Outside of my work, I use palmistry every day to give me more information to relate comfortably to people I meet.

When I sit with a client in person, I use astrology, palmistry, tarot, and runes to direct my intuition, counsel my clients, and walk with them through the twists and turns of their life. I find astrology describes the overarching patterns of the soul and the influences of this moment; palmistry describes character and the consequences of choices; and tarot and runes allow us to talk to the archetypes and look down each possible way at a crossroads in order to make informed decisions.

In *Everyday Palmistry* I share with you my accessible, open, and practical system of palmistry, distilled from my decades of experience. It is easily integrated into your daily life to deepen your understanding of the people you meet. Basic palmistry can be helpful to the clerk, body worker, politician, therapist, employer, and lover alike.

For those who want to move beyond basic palmistry to become a professional palmist, this book lays a solid foundation in an understandable and memorable format. For those who just want to know more about themselves, this approach to palmistry offers a visual portrait of our soul's patterns; it can help us to accept exactly who we are and give us clues about how to bring our lives into greater balance.

Every palmist begins to develop his or her own system, metaphors for understanding personality through the shape, form, and lines of the hand. This is mine, informed by all the hands I've seen over 30 years' experience. Try it for yourself—look at the hands of people whom you know and love, test out the theories, and see what works for you.

TERMINOLOGY

I have made some changes in traditional nomenclature that you may need to translate for further studies. Traditional palmistry books call each section of the finger a phalange, which technically means a digital bone. I use the word "section" instead, because I am not just referring to the bone.

As well as a palmist, I am an astrologer. I see the reflection between the two, but I have found that these two disciplines work better if I let each one offer its own information. Some palmists have worked hard to marry the systems and find all the details of the chart reflected on the hand. While this may be helpful to a fully fledged astrologer, I have not found it helpful to new palmists.

I use astrology to map the choices with which we were born, the structure of a person's life, her place in time and space, and her resonance with the big universal patterns. Palmistry is personal; it reflects personality, family patterns, and daily choices. It lets me see what someone is doing with the potential of her chart.

But I can't go against the priorities of astrology. Traditionally, the ring finger is called the finger of Apollo, or the Sun, and the ball of the thumb is called the mount of Venus, but I switched their names. The Sun is so huge that it would take 1.3 million Earths to match its size. It is the source of heat, light, and life on our planet. Why would all that be connected just to one of four fingers? I see the Sun's role echoed in the thumb, that expression of will that helped us humans to evolve. The ball of the thumb reflects our root energy, our internal sun. It is correlated to our sexuality as our health and physical energy reflect in our sex drive, not as our Venusian sense of romance might do.

For that we look to the ring finger, the mount underneath the ring finger, and the line heading toward the ring finger. That finger is the bearer of a wedding ring and marriage dreams, and reflector of all things Venusian—creativity, charisma, romance, and personal relationships. While this makes sense to me, if you choose to study further, you will need to translate and transpose these two mounts. Try the theories for yourself, and see what works for you.

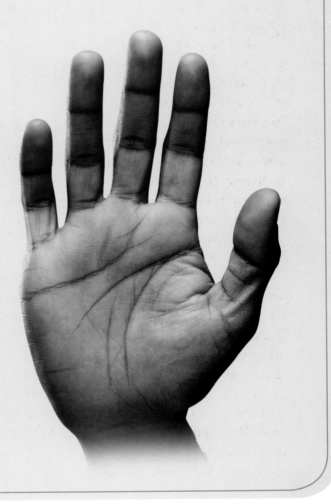

PART I

THE LANDSCAPE OF THE HAND

"What we call our destiny is truly our character and that character can be altered. The knowledge that we are responsible for our actions and attitudes does not need to be discouraging, because it also means that we are free to change this destiny. One is not in bondage to the past, which has shaped our feelings, to race, inheritance, background. All this can be altered if we have the courage to examine how it formed us. We can alter the chemistry provided we have the courage to dissect the elements." Anaïs Nin

CHARACTER AS THE FOUNDATION OF OUR HISTORY

Our hands are our energy conduits to the world. All we do and all we express with our hands become imprinted upon them. Their patterns describe how we give and receive energy and information. Our palms become our own personal mural; we paint our lines with our life history.

What we see in a hand does not define or limit the future—it describes our disposition and our disposition creates our future. We don't see the results of outside events. For example, a car accident caused by another's driving may not show up on a future line, but one caused by driving while texting might. We see the consequences of our decisions and our behavior, if we stay on the road we're now traveling.

Our hands don't change quickly or easily once we are adults, but they do evolve with our soul's progress. The mounts, the rolling landscape of our hand, change as we develop different aspects of our personality and parts of our musculature. If we use our hands in a new and different way, the bones can shift and change the line-up of the fingers. Our lines shrink or grow as we change our responses, make major decisions, develop or diffuse our life force. If, for example, a person begins to drink heavily, a network of fine lines begins to form on the hand, which diffuses the energy of the major lines, but if that person begins to live in a healthy and self-directed way, those major lines strengthen while the fine interrupting lines often fade away.

OUR PUBLIC HANDS—HOW TO USE THIS BOOK

ABOVE: We can read people from their handshake alone. The person on the left is likely to have good common sense, seen in the long lower section of the thumb, and a competent attitude, shown by the healthy musculature of the hands, and also an intuitive nature, indicated by strong, smooth fingers with smooth knuckles and skin. The person on the right is sensitive and receptive, shown by the pointed fingertips and refined skin, but has strong, pragmatic willpower—note that the top section of the thumb is broader than the base, and the thumbnail is rectangular and wide.

We can garner a lot of information from the public hand, that is the hand we see as we watch a person talk or hand us change over the counter. In Part 2 we will look at the lines and details of the hands we see only when we have permission to hold them and peer intimately. But all those details must be interpreted in the light of the basic personality, and that you can see in the public hand.

The terms we use to describe elements of palmistry are all relative, so right now, begin to notice hands. Even before you know what to look for, notice gesture, musculature, the size of hands in proportion to the body. Watch people talk with their hands or hold an object. When you shake someone's hand, notice its shape, the texture of the skin, and how firm is the handshake. Comments such as "soft" hands or "small" hands or "wide-spaced fingers" won't make sense until you begin to notice all the variations in the hands around you.

Then read this first section to learn what to look for in the landscape of the hand. Some of the information will seem like common sense, and you may realize you already notice these things. Take notes about the hands of people you know and love. Think about how these people approach the world and express their feelings, and begin to notice the relationship between the texture, shape, proportion, and bend of the hand, and what you know about their personality and life. Then all the commentary in this and other palmistry books will easily make sense.

Take this new understanding and look at the hands of people you meet, and people you work with but don't know very well yet. Develop a theory from what you observe of their hands, and then watch to see who they really are. Hands may surprise you. They may show you sides of a person that you had no idea about; we humans are so complex. So look at hands without judgment but with great curiosity. Remember that we are all a curious mix of skills and gaps, interests and blind spots. How we use our skills or minimize our deficits is our soul's choice; we can always make the most of what we have.

An organic disease, such as a connective-tissue disorder, or injury will invalidate or modify the description, so ask before jumping to conclusions. The person in question may have a healed broken bone or arthritis rather than be a stiff-necked personality.

ABOVE: This direct, clear-thinking person reaches out to shake your hand. Notice the strong, uncluttered lines on a muscle-toned hand with fine skin. He exudes healthy physical vitality, even sensuality—seen in a long and healthy life line that arches out with enthusiasm—but also sensitivity; the palm is concave, and we can see the tendons, while the fingertips flatten, even though the nails are large. This is a sensible, independent thinker. The head line is strong and level, and breaks away from the life line at an early stage.

FIRST IMPRESSIONS

The size, flexibility, color, and texture of a hand

The hands can be seen as an opening for the energy of the mind and body. The relative proportion of the hand doesn't describe the quality or quantity of our energy; it does describe how easy it is for us to pour that energy into the world. The muscle tone of the hand describes the muscularity of our engagement with the world. Do we engage with our heart and mind, or do we engage with actions, or both?

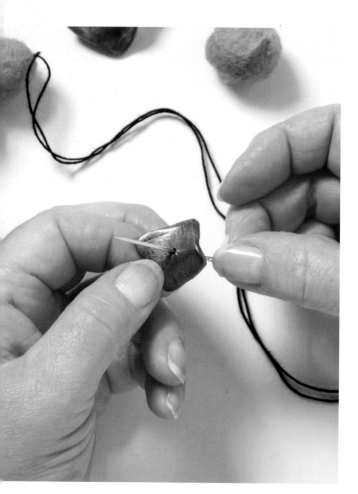

SIZE AND TONE

Large hands in proportion to the body show energetic physical engagement with the world. The owner tends to be an extrovert who has a can-do attitude. Friendliness from large-handed people may just be their way; it may not be personal. When they are angry, they may want to get physical and chop wood, hit a wall, or throw a plate. If a person with large hands has strong muscle tone, don't ask him to sit still, give him a job to do instead. Large soft hands may indicate a more passive affability. These people care but may be less active in response.

LEFT: Smallish hands with muscular fingers and slightly pointed endings suggest a friendly, creative person who can handle detailed work. She has a sociable personality, seen in her rounded fingernails. The short but strong top section of the thumb indicates that she does not like to be pushed around, nor to push others around, while the long, thick bottom section of the thumb means she has strong common sense and steady habits. She appreciates tradition but can also be stubborn.

Small hands in relation to the body tend to show a more introverted personality, someone who has condensed, internal energy. These people are thinkers who need time to consider their actions. They can be as competent as large-handed people, but with more focus and less energy expenditure. Small soft hands indicate someone who keeps a lot within, for better or worse. Those with small muscular hands can be detailed planners, thinkers, and craftspeople.

FLEXIBILITY

Notice how hands move and bend. Are the owners flexible in hand and soul?

Flexible hands can show adaptable, malleable people. Extreme flexibility can show a disposition that is hard to pin down. These people can be so chameleon-like that they reflect their surroundings to the point where it's hard to get a bead on who they really are or what they really believe.

Stiff hands come about with age. As we get older, our hands grow stiffer and we become more focused and more set in our ways. Look at where the stiffness sits. If it's in the root of the hand, it reflects a fundamental approach to life, and may be built by years of working in the same way, because it gets the job done. Stiffness in the fingers can show people are more focused and strong about their approach to life, but less flexible in their thinking.

ABOVE: These are the flexible wrists of a fundamentally adaptable person who probably travels well and easily takes to new situations and foreign cultures. She handles unexpected events with pragmatism—indicated by the thin but long bottom section to the thumb, and wide, square thumbnail.

COLOR AND TEXTURE

Feel the warmth of the hand, and note the color of the palm in comparison to overall skin tone.

Is the person hot-blooded and prone to passionate engagement? The hands will tend to show red undertones for skin type. Or is the person as cool as a cucumber, more reserved and a little harder to activate? Notice paler tones, perhaps with a blue cast, relative to skin. If the hands are noticeably cool, take it as a working hypothesis that so is this person's disposition, but do not assume it is so—health conditions may interfere with circulation.

Thin skin on the hand echoes a thin-skinned personality, someone who feels everything acutely, and may be seen by the world as too sensitive. These people may be averse to roughness or harshness and seem effete in their choices of food, textures, and surroundings, but they are honestly affected by their environment.

Coarse and thick skin may show an emotionally thicker hide, someone who can boldly wade in where angels fear to tread. These people don't react quickly to the opinions of others and so tend to stay on course whatever the feedback. They usually do not like clutter, and their tastes encompass bold statements with clean, simple lines, rather than anything subtle or fancy.

Hairiness on the back of the hands brings in a primal energy. Primal energy is strong, direct, and must be harnessed with consciousness. So look for evidence of talent or awareness in other places on the hand as a way to integrate and channel this primal energy.

The best artists have a combination of refined elements and signals of access to primal energy— the tension between these elements can produce that notorious artistic temperament. An example would be coarse hair on the back of fine skin, or low-arched fingerprints on long and delicate fingertips, or square and strong hands, with a strong thumb and mount of the Sun, and clear, graceful lines.

LEFT: It would be good for this person to have a creative outlet for his strong emotions, sensitivity, and reactiveness, which has primal undertones. Note the refined skin on muscular hands with coarse hair growing toward the knuckles. He wouldn't want to hurt anyone. He values friendship and interpersonal connections and may try to keep his feelings inside, as shown by his small fingernails, which all have a rounded base.

PROPORTION

As on the hand, so in the personality

Come to know the geometry of the hand and you can understand, rather than memorize, all the combinations. Know where to look, know what to look for, and you can figure out the rest.

DIFFERENCE BETWEEN RIGHT HAND AND LEFT

The non-dominant or passive hand shows what we came into this life with—problems we were born with or born into, skills left unused, our reserves, and our history.

The dominant or active hand is the one we use to express our mind through writing and eye-hand coordination. It shows how we have changed and what we're doing with what we came in with at birth. This hand usually changes more often because it shows the effect of our lifestyle choices, the results of our work, or new problems we face.

If possible, compare the two hands to see the changes wrought by life and life choices. If a problem resides on the non-dominant but not on the dominant hand, the person overcame it or made changes necessary to prevent it from happening. If the dominant hand has clearer and cleaner lines, the owner is growing calmer and improving her lot. If the lines are more static-filled, the major lines shorter and fainter, she may want to reconsider lifestyle choices and ask what will help her to return to innate health.

If the active hand is more dilute or looks more disoriented, she has not been able to coalesce her talent yet. Look for signs of talent, ability, and skills etched on the non-dominant but not on the dominant hand, showing untapped potential and resources she can use to improve her future.

Ambidextrous people may show less difference between the hands, as they express their thoughts and nervous energy through both, but even a fully ambidextrous person will tend to favor one hand over the other to write or to catch, and that hand will tend to show more about her present state.

THREE REALMS

Look at the three divisions of the hand—these are called realms. (Later, we will see these same patterns echoed in the three divisions of the thumb and fingers—see pages 40 and 52.) The realms start from the wrist and work upward.

THE FOUNDATIONAL REALM describes our earthy, manifest, pragmatic, material world, our root strength.

THE WORLDLY MIDDLE REALM describes our social-professional story, where most of our human interaction occurs.

THE MENTAL-EXTENSION REALM describes how we think of ourselves and the world, how we express, intuit, sense, and receive information.

Notice how large these divisions are in proportion to one another by length and width. This concept is about proportion within the hand, not comparison with other people's hands. The proportion of each realm compared with the other realms correlates to the proportions of importance to the person. Do not put a value judgment on the proportions. Don't think that it's best to look spiritual and non-materialistic with a skinny base realm and sensitive extended fingertips. This is a common new-age mistake. Here we look for balance, wholeness, and a rounded personality. We can use any proportion for good, or choose to misuse any skill. That is our soul's choice.

Also, our hands are rarely a pure type. Most hands will appear somewhere on the continuum.

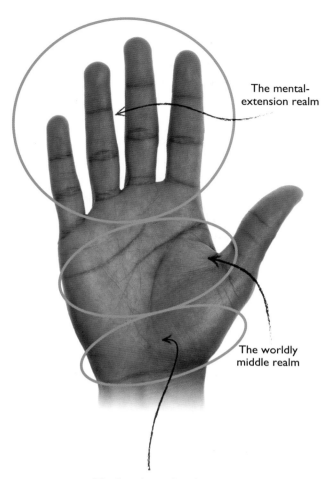

The mental-extension realm

The worldly middle realm

The foundational realm

Over time, and looking at a lot of hands, you will recognize the difference. If a realm or section is unremarkable because it's so well-proportioned with the rest, then balance is a strong resource for this person.

BASE OF THE PALM—OUR FOUNDATIONAL REALM

A hefty and substantial foundation of the palm implies physical resources, connection to the natural world, senses, and desire for material goods. It comes with a certain kinesthetic genius and sensuality. The owner values matter, can work with it beautifully, and knows the value of money and effort. She may also want to possess and hold on to stuff and people. We can see a substantial foundation realm on the palms of many natural athletes, craftspeople, laborers, engineers and mechanics, massage therapists and body healers, and on business people who have a knack for making money.

The more substantial the base of the palm is in comparison with the rest of the hand, the stronger the tendency to gather and hold on to resources, in terms of both energy and material goods. We need to look at the rest of the hand to see how this person uses the gift of earthy connectedness.

To balance: This energy can be used to build and heal, share resources, and explore the realm of ideas.

A narrowed, V-shaped base of the hand can signify someone with fewer reserves who may often tire easily, or who runs on nerves rather than strength. She may live in her social-professional or mental realms, or may be ungrounded and not pay much attention to material resources, such as money, bills, or health. She may exist somewhere between an absent-minded professor, ascetic mystic, and underfed artist. The more underfleshed this part of the hand, the stronger the tendency to honor other realms but ignore the physical, and therefore this person may have trouble creating a healthy vessel for body, finances, and relationships.

To balance: Healthy exercise is needed to build up physical reserves, and earthy matters should be attended to in a timely way. This person should try to enjoy her own physicality, and keep her life grounded.

RIGHT: This hand has a substantial, well-padded square base with square fingernails. Its owner is practical and earthy at his core and in his expression. He likes the material world, and is probably a competent mechanic, although he may be self-indulgent—he likes his comfort foods and a pint of beer. Do not try to appeal to his finer nature or to change his mind once it is made up. Be reasonable and let him know what's in the deal for him.

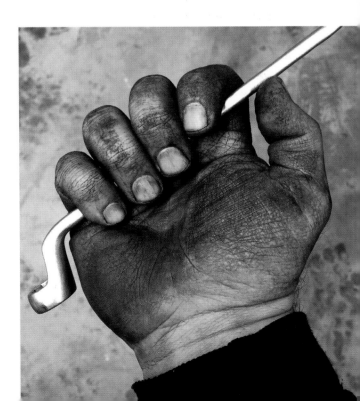

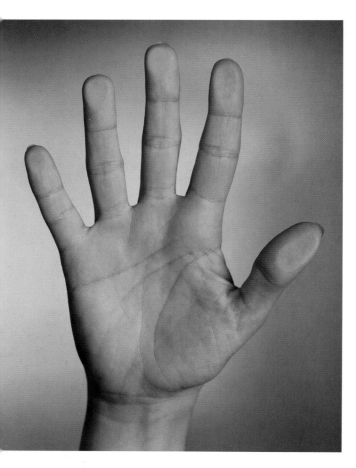

ABOVE: Note how this palm is wide and spacious at the intellectual top and earthy bottom sections, but has a sensitively narrowed and concave center, a pattern echoed by a long first and third section of the fingers, with a small and narrow midsection. This person would make a wonderful organic farmer or solar engineer. He is best approached through intellect and ideals with earthy practicality, and may not really care about professional acclaim.

MIDDLE OF THE PALM—OUR WORLDLY MIDDLE REALM

A palm that is wide across the beam—that is widest at the midsection, especially if the midsection is strong and muscular—indicates someone who puts most of her energy into human interactions, professional demeanor, and behavior in the community, group, and social milieu. This person is aware of group dynamics, and often makes a good project manager or team leader. She can successfully lead meetings or host a Thanksgiving dinner, and would like to be known as the tops in her field.

To balance: If a tree falls in the forest and no one hears it, does it make a sound? It helps to develop a sense of self-worth and investment, even if no one sees what she is doing.

A narrowed middle describes either a long thin hand with no widening in the middle, or a solidly full hand that seems perfectly rectangular with no sign of thickening or widening in the middle. This person may not care what others think. She may want just to do what she does (defined by what is strong in the hand, and she may be very good at it) and isn't worried about reputation; or she may be rather reclusive. This person may be brilliant at her craft, but it may not be a good idea to promote her to manager (unless a marked personal interest is shown) because handling the social-professional world is not her expertise.

To balance: Respect for group dynamics needs cultivating. A little more socializing would help others to gain respect for the work that she does.

TOP OF THE PALM—OUR MENTAL-EXTENSION REALM

An upward, V-shaped palm occurs when the whole palm narrows toward the base of the fingers and the fingers seem to hold more weight than the palm. This is somebody for whom ideas, concepts, and communication are enormously important. For people with this shape hand, the realm of mental activity, in either a pragmatic or metaphysical form, carries the most energy. Their antennae quiver, they can overload with the amount of information they pick up and the sensitivity with which they do it. These are innovative thinkers or people who live in their minds or imagination. Whether they are intelligent or just daydreamers is up to them. They may have a genius for communication, or they may wander in their thoughts and have trouble getting to the point. To find out whether they apply their ideas, we have to look elsewhere in the hand.

To balance: "Say less and do more" should be their mantra—walk the talk, feel feet upon the earth, and respect divinity found in the material world and in the surrounding community.

A small extension realm in proportion to the hand itself—whether this means narrow, short fingers or a hefty foundation with smaller middle and extension realms—shows intelligence. However, these people are carefully focused about how they take in information and express ideas. They will be less theoretical and more applied and specific, and may make better listeners than speakers, although when they do speak, they can get right to the point.

To balance: These people should consider the theory, philosophy, or intuitive experience behind an action, and practice safe, comfortable methods of expression.

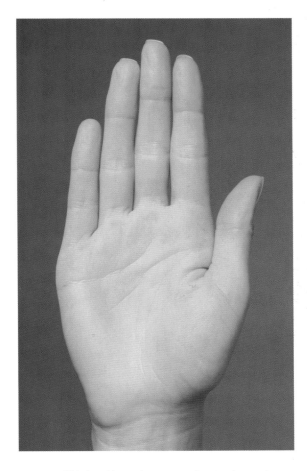

ABOVE: This hand has a large mental-extension realm. Appeal to this person's mind—he wants to understand the theory behind things, explore possibilities, and communicate effectively. Money has little hold on him. The middle and top sections of the fingers are long and substantial, with space between the fingertips for coins to slide through, echoed by the wide upper palm compared to the narrow base.

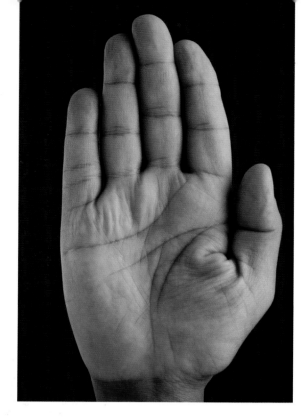

ABOVE: Notice the rounded/square palm and full mounts, and how the first and middle finger have a definite lean toward the private side of the hand. This generally practical, warm, and earthy person needs privacy and time alone, or with close family, to recharge.

WHICH WAY DO WE LEAN: OUR PRIVATE/PUBLIC METER

Most hands are directed and centered, focused toward the middle finger, which represents a balance between general introversion and extroversion, between concentration on our inner and outer realms. Bear in mind that the bones in the hand can shift during a lifetime, and the lean of the fingers and hands can change.

If the fingers and the bones tend to lean toward the little finger—toward the private side of life—this person will tend to be introverted, possibly introspective, and focused on the people she has come to trust over time.

If the fingers and bones lean toward the forefinger (also known as the pointer or index finger)—the more public part of the hand—the person will tend to be more hail fellow well met, more outgoing, outward-focused, extroverted, or interested in the public good. The more extreme is the tendency, the more likely she is to overlook the people close to her.

Fingers leaning toward the private side

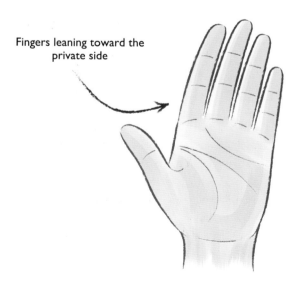

Fingers leaning toward the public side

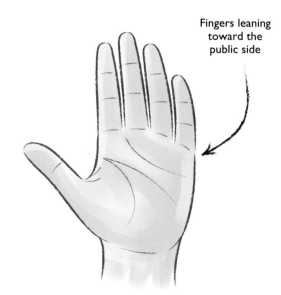

THE SHAPE OF US

Six shapes found in the palm and fingertips

The average palm is as wide as it is long, and the middle finger is about the length of the palm. Any variations on this have significance. Look first at the overall shape of the hand. Is it round, oval, square, rectangular, pointed, or spatulate? Then look for these shapes in the heel of the hand, the top of the palm, the fingertips, and the fingernails. Combine the meaning of the shape with what that particular part of the hand signifies (and we'll learn more about fingertips on pages 54–59).

In general, the width of the hand refers to our capacity to engage this earthly world of ours. The wider it is, the more solid and substantial our ability to manage the world pragmatically. The narrower the palm appears, the more a person focuses her perceptions. She may be more sensitive than others about the information coming in and going out, and so may overload if she feels barraged by stimuli.

The longer the hand, the longer a person remains in the realm of thoughts and ideas. The shorter the hand, the more a person tends to act first and think later, or simultaneously, or perhaps to keep herself to herself.

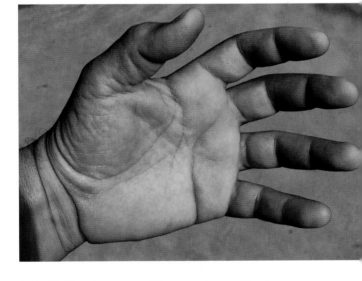

ABOVE: Give the owner of these hands something to do, and don't make him wait. He's strong-willed and pours physical energy into this world through hard work, sensuality, hunger, and pragmatic skills. Note the square, wide, firm but well-upholstered hand, with the deep physical reserves of a strong mount of the Sun. An unusually large and wide thumb suggests willfulness and a desire to follow through.

ROUND HANDS

Good at dealing with the public

A round shape implies sociability, friendliness, diplomacy, coziness, and often a caring personality, someone who puts people first. A pure type round hand is as wide as it is long, with fingers about the same length as the palm, but the round shape brings this affability wherever it shows up.

A rounded foundational realm implies someone who needs to get along with the people she lives and works with, who prefers to keep close to community. This person would be unhappy taking a scientific job in the Arctic, for example, where she would be stuck, cut off from others for long periods. Human interaction is a fundamental need.

A rounded shape at the top of the palm shows someone who puts people first during daily interactions. If the whole palm appears circular, this is a genuinely nice person, the cozy, friendly, caring, heart of a family or community sort. Rounded at the top of the hand does not imply practical order, if the rounded arch drops off noticeably around the little finger and the little

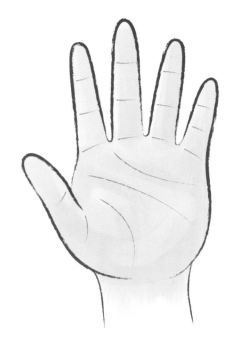

finger is set considerably lower than the ring or index fingers. This person may have a place for everything, but not everything is in its place.

If the palm appears squared off at the base but rounded at the top, this person may have a pragmatic foundation but may express herself and interact with the world in a more sociable and diplomatic way. She cares, but has a practical mindset. These pragmatic but cuddly people often make excellent therapists, teachers, diplomats, or customer-service representatives.

MELISSA McCARTHY
Comedian and actor Melissa McCarthy has the rounded hands of a person who puts relationships first, and who values kindness over practicality.

BILL CLINTON

Bill Clinton is a natural philosopher and communicator—note the long fingers and the oval palm—with pragmatic foundations (his palm's base is squared off) and a large field of action in his life (his palm has a long and wide midsection). He expresses himself with diplomacy, seen in the rounded top of the palm, and long, rounded fingertips.

OVAL/ALMOND HANDS

Good communicator

Oval hands are a subset of the rounded shape. They are rounded at the base, with a long palm that is rounded at the top, and the fingers are usually long with almond-shaped nails. Oval hands represent the sociability of the round hand with the added dimension of thoughtfulness before action that comes with the long palm and long fingers. They suggest a good, balanced, sociable, thoughtful community member. Look for oval hands on committee members, or the spokesperson for the company or the parent-teacher organization.

These people are generally good team players, but do not underestimate their intelligence and basic need to understand what's going on. They often have a great sense of aesthetics and are usually aware of the feelings of the people around them. They prefer to avoid conflict. Ask them meaningful questions but approach them as if you know there is common ground between you. The longer and thinner the hand, the more the characteristics drift into those of the pointed hand.

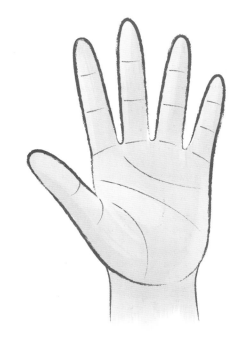

POINTED HANDS

Sensitive and perceptive

Pointed hands are long, thin, and elegant with fingers that taper distinctly. These sensitive people feel everything and are easily hurt. They may find it challenging to let go. Long thin hands receive and express much subtle information, but this person may not feel sturdy enough to take on a large social exchange. The longer and thinner the hand, the more the person exists in the realm of sensibilities and less in grounded pragmatics. She may become overwhelmed when her senses seem barraged, or when her world feels disorganized and out of control. Fine, detailed work can be a great relief to her. Point her toward the arts, healing, research, refinement, any environment where she can put her sensitivities to good use. Active artists with pointed hands may develop a noticeable public persona that takes the wear and tear of social interaction while giving them some interpersonal insulation.

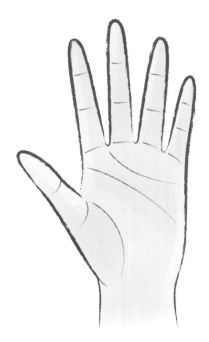

LADY GAGA

Lady Gaga (Stefani Joanne Angelina Germanotta) has a relatively small, strong palm and long, unusually pointed fingers, which suggest that she pours effort and energy into the world, but runs more on nerves than on strength. She has a huge public presence. Her palm is almost diamond-shaped, and her fingers and palm point toward Jupiter. She picks up a lot from the world, seen in her pointed fingertips, and because of that sensitivity she filters her interaction in the world through the mask of her very public persona. She has a strong ear for language and music, indicated by her unusually long Mercury finger.

SQUARE HANDS

Gets the job done

The square shape shows a fundamentally practical nature. If the foundation is square, that person is essentially practical, even if she interacts with the world in a friendly (rounded) or focused and sensitive (pointed) way. No matter how congenial she may seem, a proposal has to make practical sense, or she probably won't agree. A square upper edge of the palm suggests pragmatic organization in daily life. She wants things in their place, worktable organized, and thoughts sorted. Present information to her in a linear manner, and put the tools back where you found them.

Entirely square palms (as wide as they are tall, with angular edge corners) show extreme practicality. This person wants to see how it's done, requires sound workmanship, and needs to understand why it makes sense.

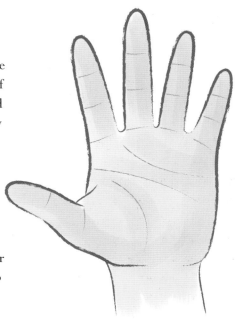

PELÉ

Famed soccer player Pelé (Edson Arantes do Nascimento) has a basically square hand, as wide as it is long, with rounded fingers and upper arch. These suggest that he has good reflexes and energy to give, yet is more sociable than many athletes—indeed, after he retired, he became a worldwide ambassador for the game.

ANGELA MERKEL

These are the hands of a no-nonsense, pragmatic person—shown by the square-based but deep, long palm—focused toward worldly engagement. Note how the palm tilts toward the mount of Jupiter and a long Jupiter finger. German politician Angela Merkel has deep reserves of good common sense, and is not easily moved from an established position, indicated by a strong mount of the Sun.

RECTANGULAR HANDS

Good investigator

Rectangular hands—squared off at the corners and longer than they are wide—are a subset of square. They take the fundamental pragmatic earthiness of the square and add the thoughtful dimension of length. Long rectangular palms suggest an intrinsically rational person who manifests her practicality in ideas and thoughts. Look for rectangular hands among scientists, engineers, entrepreneurs, politicians, and business people with fresh ideas. These people want to hear the long explanation. They are result-oriented and want the story to make sense, but also want to understand the thought process behind your conclusion. The longer the palm, the deeper and more complex their inner world. Don't mistake rationality for lack of love and empathy—this is just how they perceive and express. But when discussing a problem with a rectangular-handed person, start with the facts and add the backstory later.

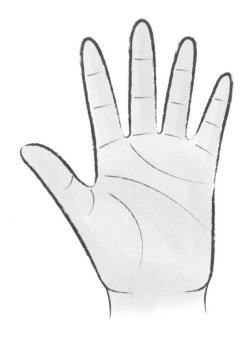

SPATULATE OR SPLAYED HANDS

Full of energy

Spatulate hands are V-shaped, usually muscular, narrow at the base and wider across the beam. The shape acts like a megaphone, magnifying the energy coming out of the hands. Don't expect people with spatulate hands to be good on detail. They are better suited to directing the movie, organizing the rescue mission, or starting up a new business. They may make healers who pour energy into their clients, or leaders who inspire the troops. They are initiators, often risk-takers, with low impulse control—if they see it, they do it. Learning patience may be a challenge for them.

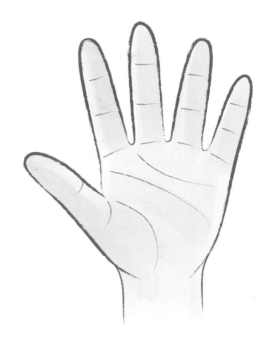

DANICA PATRICK

This successful racecar driver is a natural action star—her hand widens from the base, her fingers reach out naturally, and she has a low-set thumb. She is honest and direct, independent, and appreciates bravery, indicated by the clean and clear lines on her palm, and by the way her level head line springs away from the life line and keeps its distance from the heart line. She has spatulate hands with squared-off fingertips. Do not waste her patience, and keep matters practical with her.

THE MOUNTS OF OUR HAND

Pools of energy

*The mounts of the hand act as pools of energetic reserves, and that
energy is expressed by the fingers. Notice which mounts are prominent.
These describe the person's main points of interest and skill. Notice
which mounts are underdeveloped, indicating where some building up
needs to be done.*

My correlation of astrology with the fingers
and mounts is slightly different from what you
find in classical palmistry. I reverse Sun and
Venus, but this comes from my understanding
of astrological symbols and my decades of
comparing hands to charts. It makes sense.

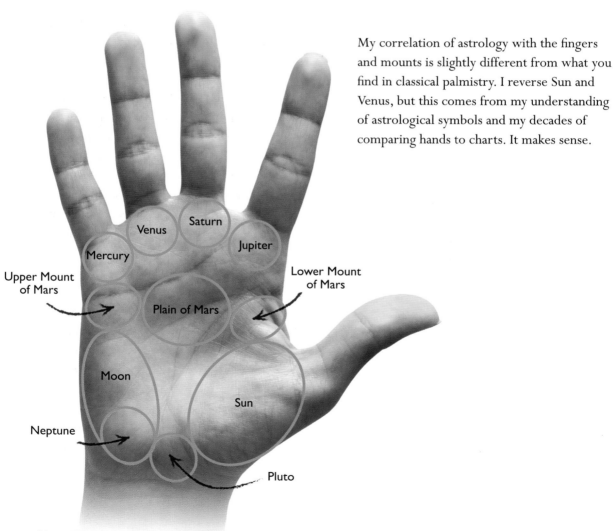

Venus

Saturn

Mercury

Jupiter

Upper Mount
of Mars

Lower Mount
of Mars

Plain of Mars

Moon

Sun

Neptune

Pluto

SUN

The mount of the Sun, the ball of the thumb, describes our reserves of Chi or physical vitality. Our Chi is the physical engine that drives the rest of the chart. The larger and fuller this mount in relation to the hand, the more its owner operates with strong physical vitality. When it seems especially large for the hand, the person may get angry quickly, have an overactive sex drive, or a good immune system but be prone to high blood pressure, or have so much energy he doesn't quite know how to deal with it. The bigger the engine, the more thoughtfully we have to drive the car.

A small mount of the Sun indicates running on nerves more than strength. This person may not be able to count on good health, and may choose a life that is not physically oriented. If you want to seduce a person with a slight Sun mount, you need to bring his mind along. Use words and images rather than count on chemistry and sex drive, although these people may have just as much fun once they get going.

To balance: Physical reserves can be built up through healthy living, exercise, and finding joy in the movement of the body.

MOON

The mount of the Moon, bottom of the palm, opposite the mount of the Sun on the percussion side of the hand, describes our unspoken psychic realm, our dream world, our deepest imagination, how we connect to the collective unconscious and to our sense of history both personal and cultural.

The fuller and more muscular the mount of the Moon, the stronger is that connection to the unconscious realms. Lines that flow up from this area unimpeded imply that we have entry to them and can drop into our connection with the collective and with our deepest imagination. A curve or bulge along the outer edge of the mount of the Moon implies an interest in, or ability to access, the resources of history. A bulge higher up implies an interest in more recent history; the lower down the bulge, the more ancient the interests.

A slight mount of the Moon, in comparison with the rest of the hand, indicates no particular interest in the imaginative or archetypal realms, and more interest in what can be seen and felt, in the present rather than the past.

To balance: Keeping a dream journal, taking a psychic development class, and researching family history are all ways to promote empathy with the more spiritual side of life.

NEPTUNE

The mount of Neptune is the bottom part of the mount of the Moon and describes the depths of our intuition and how we can connect to the collective psyche in a deep and cellular way. A well-developed mount of Neptune with many lines reaching into it suggests an active and connective intuitive or imaginary realm. There's more about the mount of Neptune in the section on the minor lines (see page 109).

MERCURY

The mount of Mercury, underneath the little finger, describes how our private thoughts work, how we analyze and diagnose problems, and how we relate to others on an intimate level. This mount is associated with sounds, and the ability to appreciate and work with words, music, and poetry.

A full and well-developed mount of Mercury shows a strongly analytical cast of mind, someone who is interested in understanding how people work, the mind-body connection, or how the psyche works. It implies a certain interpersonal shrewdness and articulation. Mercury was the messenger of the gods, but also the god of thieves, and this dichotomy describes our ability to use the mind for good or for manipulation. It's up to us.

A slight mount of Mercury suggests someone who does not naturally express himself in words or music, who might feel shy about speaking up, and who may find it challenging to negotiate his needs in a relationship.
To balance: Classes on speaking in public or in negotiation can help, as can listening to music, writing poetry, and speaking up for your needs and for what you see.

VENUS

The mount of Venus, underneath the ring finger, describes our heart, our creative process, and our intimate social relationships.

A full mount of Venus expresses a charismatic, warmhearted person, who feels respect for the creative process. When it is truly full, its owner may use a surplus of charm diplomatically, to serve with compassion or passion, or to manipulate. His heart can feel on fire.

A slight mount of Venus suggests someone who may be just as creative, but less comfortable showing his art forms. He may be just as warmhearted, but more awkward in expression. Passionate relationships may not be the driving force in his life. And you won't find him discussing art theory down at the coffeehouse.
To balance: Art classes or writing retreats may be an enjoyable step in the right direction, and joining groups in which members have clear roles can encourage social skills by building experiences of success and so confidence.

MARS

The upper and lower mounts of Mars describe how we experience and express our temper and ambition, our competitive nature, entrepreneurial streak, emotional and physical defenses, and our immune systems. The lower mount of Mars is just above the ball of the thumb and below the life line and head line. The upper mount of Mars is found in the corresponding area on the percussion side of the hand, above the mount of the Moon and below the mount of Mercury. The plain of Mars describes the center of the hand between these two mountains.

LOWER MOUNT OF MARS

This describes how we handle our temper. You can see the lower mount of Mars easily when the thumb is held alongside the hand, but you

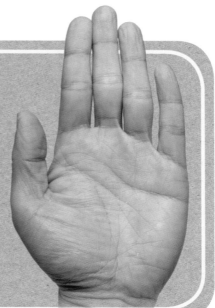

This hand has a round and sociable palm, with a strong foundation in the Sun and the Moon, but notice the space between the first section of the fingers—coins would fall through them. This is not a person who focuses on the material practicalities, and probably does let money run through his fingers. He has a good-sized Mercury mount, indicating a spacious mind, but the curve of the upper palm sets the mounts of Mercury and Venus much lower than those of Jupiter and Saturn, which suggests a mind, personal life, and desk that are not particularly organized. A kindly, creative approach is best for this person. Appeal to him with ideas, ideals, and aesthetics.

can still get a fairly clear image when the hand is waved about.

A small and flat lower mount of Mars indicates someone without much temper, who may have trouble setting boundaries, and fending off the passing cold. If it is small but muscular and flat, this shows a short, fast, hot temper that releases quickly, a reactive personality who doesn't hold on to things. This person may have overactive emotional defenses, and possibly autoimmune complications.

When the mount is large and low, this may describe someone whose temper is slow to boil but who has a long memory for apparent slights.

If it is flat and close to the life line but puffier toward the thumb, it indicates someone who is slow to boil but who holds some deep resentments within. The puffier and more developed it is, the hotter and faster the temper, and the more hair-trigger the defenses.

Expansive, muscular, and puffy shows a formidable temperament. This person can be an heroic warrior for good, or an impossible bully. Look for signs of common sense, balance, rationality, and kindliness elsewhere in the hand to guide this energy.

To balance a slight lower mount of Mars: Physical energy needs building up, perhaps by taking a martial-arts course, such as tai chi or aikido. This also provides an active physical metaphor for healthy ways to deflect unwanted people or germs, a defense of peaceful strength.

To balance an overdeveloped lower mount of Mars: That force for good can be channeled into being a warrior for the people, a protector and defender. Anger-management classes may be of benefit, as will learning to count to five before responding.

UPPER MOUNT OF MARS

This describes our ambition, stability of purpose, mental resilience, and self-control.

A well-developed mount imbues cool competence, entrepreneurial qualities, and a distinctly adventurous edge. People with a noticeably developed mount of Mars can be fiercely ambitious in their fields of interest. They hate to lose, and can push themselves hard to be the best.

To balance a slight upper mount of Mars: Self-confidence is to be encouraged, as is belief in personal competence, perhaps through education and learning practical skills, followed by venturing outside the comfort zone and taking the next safe step toward adventure.

To balance an overdeveloped upper mount of Mars: All that confidence and capability can be poured into charitable work.

PLAIN OF MARS

This is the large section in the middle of the hand between the two mounts, the part where all the lines cross. The plain of Mars describes our willingness to engage in the playing field or battleground of life. Most of us have an unremarkable plain of Mars; it's just the campus upon which the lines play.

If it is thin-skinned, enough to see the tendons easily, it means this person may be so sensitive that he backs away from the hustle and bustle of life. He may be wildly talented but prefer not to compete, and may like to work away from the fray. It may look as though these people are not living up to their potential, but they need to find a way to engage with the world that feels comfortable and safe to them.

A strong, wide, and muscular plain shows a person who dives in to the competition and engages life with both hands.

A puffy midsection as part of a hand that is overall padded and soft shows someone who has insulated himself and who may take more of a gourmand rather than gourmet approach to life.

JUPITER

The mount of Jupiter, under the forefinger, signifies strength for dealing with the world at large and describes the energy we direct toward our public persona, our ability to teach, present, and reach out.

A full and strong mount of Jupiter with the finger curving toward the little finger or with a well-developed mount of the Moon shows someone who may need time alone to renew, but who can still be comfortable reaching out. A strong mount of Jupiter increases charisma, positivity, enthusiasm, and the capacity to be a public figure.

When the mount is slight, this implies someone for whom dealing with people he does not know, or being visible out in the world, can be challenging, taking a lot away without giving much back.

To balance: Confidence in public interaction must be built in a safe and gentle way, possibly through teaching a favorite subject, even to just a few people at a time, or working in a group for a good cause or spiritual practice.

SATURN

The mount of Saturn, underneath the middle finger, is usually flat, owing to the musculature of the hand. It is the balancing pivot point of the hand and speaks of our philosophical reserves, our efforts to balance our inner world with our outer world, our personal world with our public world. It speaks of our relationship to authority, our own and other people's, and our relationship to tradition.

A proportionally large Saturn mount reflects natural personal authority, and the philosophical bent of someone who carefully weighs conflicting concerns and personal needs and the needs of others. Taken to an extreme, he could become stuck in the morass of philosophic angst and prone to being morose or saturnine.

If the mount of Saturn is slight or unmarked, this shows someone who may not be interested in such philosophical blathering. He may spend less time thinking about what needs to be done and more time doing it.

To balance: Someone with a slight mount of Saturn needs to take personal responsibility, hold himself responsible for his happiness and not look for outside excuses. It would be helpful if he could contemplate why he does what he does.

Note the large but relatively flat upper mount of Mars, which suggests a slow-boil temper. This is someone who doesn't anger easily and may not express her temper comfortably. She may therefore have trouble working out disagreements, and hold on to problems for a long time. Notice that her heart line is deep (see page 81)— it reaches toward the space between the Saturn and Jupiter fingers, but never quite reaches the edge. This person may get a lot out of both her personal and professional relationships, but rarely takes the initiative to grow intimacy. This distance may be exacerbated by memories of earlier hurts or resentment that she didn't have a chance to clear. If you want to get close to her, you need to reach out. A square palm (as wide as it is long) and a square top of the palm (note that all the fingers start on a relative line) indicate an organized, logical manner. She is most comfortable in the practical and logical realm.

PLUTO

Between the mount of the Moon and the mount of the Sun, at the very bottom of the hand, is usually an indentation from which the fate line rises. This is the mount of Pluto and it describes the sense of personal empowerment and soul strength we develop by handling our life. It indicates our ability to keep to our own rhythm, even around powerful people.

A full mount of Pluto signifies unconscious personal power, for better or for worse.

A deeper dent in this area may describe a person who felt powerless early on in life, or has faced some truly disempowering obstacles.

Note the difference between the dominant and non-dominant hand to see if the person was born that way, or has developed his sense of personal empowerment over time.

To balance: Someone with a slight mount of Pluto should learn to beat his own drum—take note of the times in life when he took back power from willful people and made good decisions.

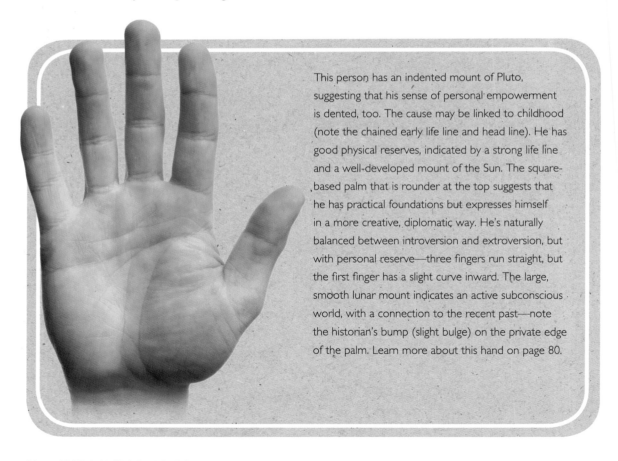

This person has an indented mount of Pluto, suggesting that his sense of personal empowerment is dented, too. The cause may be linked to childhood (note the chained early life line and head line). He has good physical reserves, indicated by a strong life line and a well-developed mount of the Sun. The square-based palm that is rounder at the top suggests that he has practical foundations but expresses himself in a more creative, diplomatic way. He's naturally balanced between introversion and extroversion, but with personal reserve—three fingers run straight, but the first finger has a slight curve inward. The large, smooth lunar mount indicates an active subconscious world, with a connection to the recent past—note the historian's bump (slight bulge) on the private edge of the palm. Learn more about this hand on page 80.

THUMB AND FINGERS

Our conduits of expression and perception

The thumb and fingers show how we express the root energy of the mount, and how we receive information along those same lines. You could almost think of them as similar to a row of taps at a bar, each one channeling a different draft.

Get a general impression of the fingers and then look at each one individually. Notice if the conduit is wide and deep or narrow and focused—how thick and how long is each section in relation to the others?

Note anything particularly unusual. For instance, if a nice round hand with rounded fingers has a squared-off first finger, that person is much more pragmatic in his approach to the public than he is to the rest of life.

For each section, or realm (see page 40), and each whole finger, the length interpreted in relationship to the hand maps where a person has inherent talent, and this is important in developing skill. The width shows earthiness or practicality. If fingers are muscular, that indicates a pragmatic doer; if they are soft, that person has a love of comfort or a more emotional and less physical approach to life; if fingers are really soft and wide, it hints at indulgence or even gluttony.

Length of section	Significance	Width of section	Significance
short	unimportant or underdeveloped	thin and bony	idealistic, ascetic, unembodied
medium	balanced/unremarkable	medium	balanced/unremarkable
long	important	full but muscular	pragmatic worker
		thick but puffy	passive/indulgent

THE THUMB

The thumb describes willpower and common sense, and can express our physical energy. Our vitality is symbolically stored in the ball of the thumb, which is the mount of the Sun (see page 31) and also the first realm of the thumb (see page 40). Our versatile opposable thumb is one of the great evolutionary advances of being human, a way to work our human will on the world, for better or worse.

The average thumb is set about halfway between the forefinger and the wrist, and extends to halfway up the first section of the forefinger. If the thumb varies from this setting, it may be because the thumb is unusually large or small, or set unusually high or low on the hand.

A large thumb shows a strong-minded, willful, and charismatic person, an alpha type and potential leader, but whether for good or ill is up to him. These people do not naturally follow orders, and have to believe in the goal if they are to cooperate.

A small thumb suggests a more receptive or beta personality, someone who may choose to cooperate, or to work on his own, rather than lead others in an adventure. These people are wonderful on a team because they won't push or pull too much and can get the work done, but they may become overwhelmed if put on the spot or inundated with too many variables at the same time.

A high-set thumb, closer to the forefinger, shows a person who tends to resist change and is less prone to finding ingenious solutions. A very small and high-set thumb may point to developmental issues.

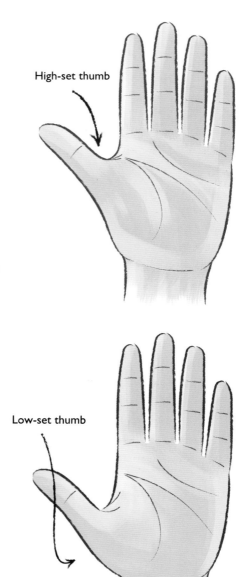

High-set thumb

Low-set thumb

A low-set thumb, closer to the wrist, shows a person who handles life in an independent, opinionated, can-do, but sometimes manipulative, way.

ANGLE OF THE THUMB

This is an indicator of generosity and willingness to engage. When you ask people to hold out their hands, most people naturally hold the thumb at a 45° angle, but this changes depending on how we feel about our circumstances at the time.

Holding the thumb closer to the hand shows caution about expressing will or extending financial or personal resources. The wider the angle, the more likely a person is to be hands-on, ready for the job, ready to use will and resources to achieve a goal. A larger than 90° angle shows a propensity to spend resources unwisely and willfully engage the world whether that is what's wanted or not.

When someone hides his thumb, walking around with the fist wrapped around it, he may be feeling an internal struggle about expressing a strong primitive emotion and he may have his own good reasons for this. Be very careful about interfering. If this is a quiet, meek person, he may have been trained not to express his opinions and possibly could use some encouragement, but once he gets going you may be deluged. Alternatively, a large-handed, energetic person may be trying to contain strong emotions. Leave him be.

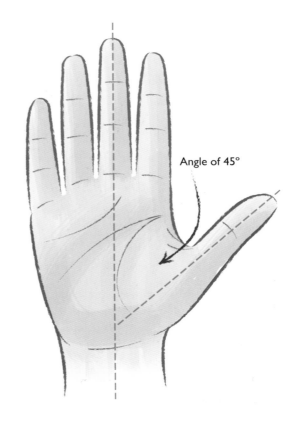

Angle of 45°

RIGHT: Here we see strong thumbs—long and wide in proportion to the hand, suggesting that this person is much more stubborn and determined than she first appears. Her hands are wide, with a thick first section of each finger. This person is good with materials, rather indulgent in creature comforts, and may bargain well, indicated by the long first and second finger sections and relatively short third sections. This is not a theoretical person—approach her pragmatically.

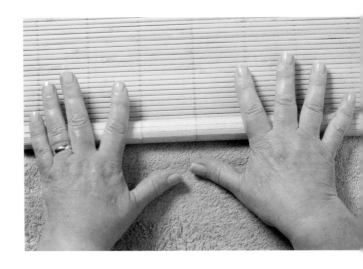

REALMS OF THE THUMB

As with the hand and fingers, the thumb is divided into three sections, or realms. Look especially at the proportion between the second and third realms. They are usually about the same and since they represent common sense and will, it is good to have that balance between the two.

THE FIRST REALM: The ball of the thumb is considered to be the thumb's first realm as well as the mount of the Sun.

THE SECOND REALM: This indicates the practicality with which we express our will, impulse control, and our ability to fit in with standard rules. A short second realm implies that common sense isn't that important to this person, and may be something he needs to develop. A long second realm implies that common sense is so

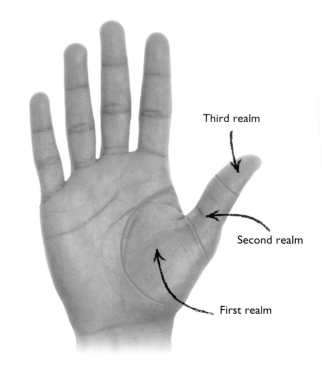

Third realm

Second realm

First realm

strong, it can be hard to express spontaneously. If the second is longer than the third realm, the owner has more won't power than willpower. Great natural stubbornness can lead him to dig in his heels and stick with tradition, and he may have trouble breaking away to instigate a new phase.

A wide second realm means common sense is shown in a pragmatic, earthy, mechanical way. If it's narrow, common sense is more intellectual and reasoned, but may not be materially practical.

THE THIRD REALM: This indicates our willpower. The larger and more bulbous the thumb, the more impulsive is its owner, and the more inclined to express an opinion and affect the world. The smaller this realm, the less he wants to assert himself or impose his will on the world.

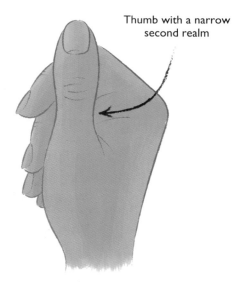

Thumb with a narrow second realm

A clubbed thumb is formed when the second realm is short and thin while the third realm is large and bulbous. It indicates a lot of willpower, not particularly controlled by any common sense or desire to fit in with the pack. This has been called a murderer's thumb, but not everyone with this type of thumb is dangerous! Someone with a clubbed thumb may be charismatic and energetic but have trouble controlling impulses. This is someone who could lose his temper.

To balance: Someone with a clubbed thumb would find it helpful to develop impulse control, common sense, and the compassion to be responsible for his own actions.

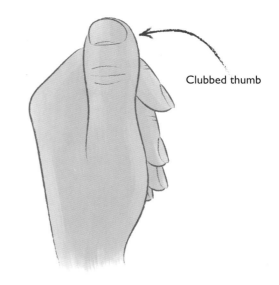

Clubbed thumb

If you see a distinct difference between someone's two hands, as in the thumbnails here, first ask if this is the result of an accident of some kind. If not, the characteristics of both hands should be considered. In this case, the thumb of the right hand has a much shorter nail and top section than the thumb of the left. This suggests that a certain experience, probably early on in this person's life, stunted her ability to know and express her own will. Check the life line for signs of early trauma or oppression (see page 64). She has solid common sense, indicated by the wide bottom section of her thumbs, but may have trouble truly knowing what she wants and is aiming for.

FINGERS

Fingers delineate how we sense our world and how we express ourselves. They show us what parts of our life take up a lot of our time, what is less important to us, where we are ascetic, and where we are indulgent. In palmistry, the fingers are named the same as the mounts of the hand (see page 30): the forefinger is Jupiter, the middle finger is Saturn, the ring finger is Venus and the little finger is Mercury. We'll find out more about each finger on pages 44–51.

First look at the proportions of the fingers. Which ones are longer or shorter in comparison with the others? Look at the knuckles, the length of each section in relationship to the others, the shape and color of the nails. Later we'll examine the fingerprints (possibly with the aid of a magnifying glass).

On the average hand, the middle finger, or Saturn, is the longest, with the two fingers on either side, Jupiter and Venus, coming up to approximately the middle of the top section. The little finger, Mercury, reaches to about the joint between the second and third sections on the ring finger. If you see a variation on this, look at how the fingers are set, and check to see if one finger is actually longer than the other, or if it just appears that way because of the curve of the hand. The positions of the bones can change over a person's lifetime and so the proportions between the fingers can appear to shift, and the personality follows suit.

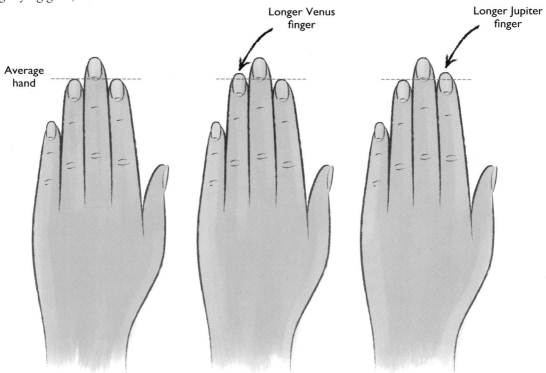

Average hand

Longer Venus finger

Longer Jupiter finger

KNUCKLES

Be aware that knobby knuckles may be the result of arthritis rather than indicative of anything else. Smooth knuckles speak of an intuitive or instinctive responsiveness; knotty knuckles of a philosophical rigor or doubting mind, indicating someone who wants to understand before speaking or acting. This person has to see something work before he believes in it.

People whose fingers are smooth through the upper knuckle but with a pronounced, knotty knuckle below pick up information by intuition and sensory awareness, and then scrutinize it with logic or doubt. Yes, our knuckles get more pronounced as we age, and so does our logic and desire for competence in others.

ABOVE: These appear to be the hands of someone who is young, judging by the skin, and philosophic or scientific. The prominent knuckles imply a well-developed sense of intellectual rigor or an argumentative mind. The long, thin fingers suggest a person who likes to work in depth; the spaces between the base of the fingers, together with long first and second sections, suggest a more mental and less physical approach to life. A long, thin thumb indicates willpower and common sense, someone who does not like to be imposed upon, but equally does not like to impose her will on others.

THE JUPITER FINGER

The forefinger expresses our most public self, our dealings with the world at large, and how we react in a group of people.

A long and strong Jupiter finger is connected with confidence, ambition, extroversion, and ease in front of a crowd. Someone with a very long Jupiter finger can appear overconfident or arrogant, or be so attached to his public persona that he has trouble taking off the mask.

A strong Jupiter finger that has an overall bend toward the middle finger indicates someone who has good leadership abilities but is fairly introspective and may be wary of being overexposed. Such people often make thoughtful, considered speakers, but they may prefer not to talk to a packed stadium, or if they do, they need solitude afterward.

A Jupiter finger with a sharp bend at the top knuckle may show indirect or passive aggression.

A short Jupiter finger can mean insecurity or lack of confidence in the world. In a mildly muscle-toned hand, this may indicate a retiring disposition. In a muscular hand, it may indicate a drive to prove oneself and overcompensate for this insecurity. Over time, and with growing confidence, the bones can shift in the hand and the Jupiter finger can appear to lengthen.

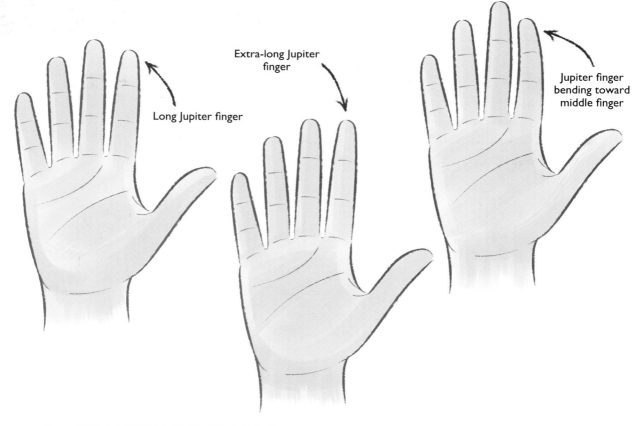

Long Jupiter finger

Extra-long Jupiter finger

Jupiter finger bending toward middle finger

RICHARD BRANSON

These hands indicate a confident, competent public person who takes a global perspective, acting with bravado, and whose eye is always on expansion and success. His Jupiter finger is long, almost as long as his Saturn finger, and his hands are long and muscular. He pours energy into his surroundings and thinks in terms of the big picture more than details (his fingernails are much wider than they are long, with squared fingertips). But the privacy of his personal life is essential—his strong Jupiter finger curves toward his Saturn finger—so don't ask personal questions when the camera is on.

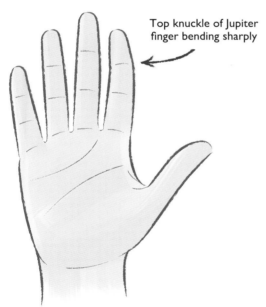

Top knuckle of Jupiter finger bending sharply

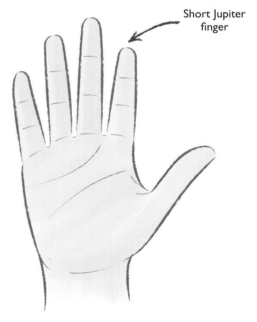

Short Jupiter finger

ABOVE: The Saturn finger here is slightly curved on the first knuckle, but more so on the lower knuckle—she tends to feel stress in her gut. These long fingers with mildly knotty knuckles suggest a careful thinker who perceives intuitively and likes order in her environment.

THE SATURN FINGER

The middle finger is our finger of personal authority and philosophy. It expresses how we worry about or balance our inner and outer worlds, and is the finger we gesture with rudely as a way of asserting our authority and opinion. On either side of our balance post (middle finger) are Jupiter's finger (forefinger), which shows how we express ourselves in the outer world, and the Venus finger (ring finger), which shows how we express ourselves in our more personal world.

A long finger of Saturn indicates someone who makes an effort to understand the bigger picture, to develop a philosophy that helps him balance inner and outer worlds. The possessor of an exceptionally long middle finger is a worrier who is always poking and prodding his concerns. He may have a melancholic or saturnine disposition, and have a hard time taking the world on faith.

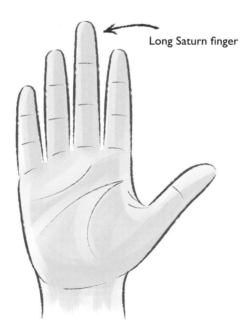

Long Saturn finger

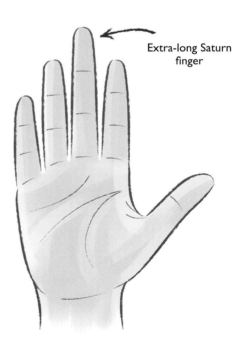

Extra-long Saturn finger

A short middle finger shows someone who tends to be pragmatic but who may not naturally stand back to get things into perspective. This may be because he doesn't think things through before he speaks or takes action, or because he feels that to philosophize is not enough—one must act.

Our worry easily affects our health, and this shows up on the middle finger. If the Saturn finger bends to the side at the top knuckle, the person tends to feel stress in the head, shoulders, or respiratory system. If the Saturn finger bends at the second knuckle, stress is felt in the gut.

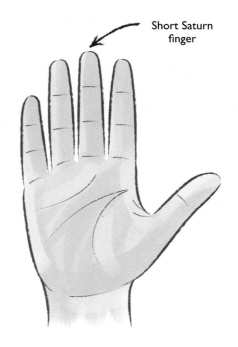

Short Saturn finger

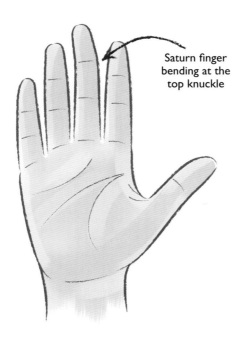

Saturn finger bending at the top knuckle

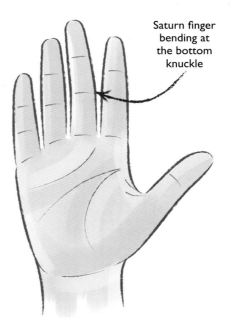

Saturn finger bending at the bottom knuckle

THE VENUS FINGER

The Venus finger mirrors the Jupiter finger in our personal world. It describes our personal relationships, friendships, and creative process. When we marry, tradition has us put a ring on this finger, on the left, more private hand (and on the first, or the physical, section) suggesting that in marriage we limit what we do in the physical realm of our private social life.

A long Venus finger suggests that this is someone for whom the social world is important. People with a long Venus finger may be charismatic or part of the glue that holds the community together. They take a creative approach to life and have an emotionally passionate nature—visual people who notice aesthetics and need beauty to live. Their success may come from charm, creative problem-solving, or optimism.

A noticeably long, substantial Venus finger can indicate a romancer, compulsive artist, collector, adventurer, or gambler, someone who has trouble knowing when to stop.

A slight Venus finger—one that is thin or waisted compared with the other fingers—indicates that its owner is probably not a social animal, and may need others to reach out to him. This is someone who doesn't necessarily value the artistic process. A thoroughly underdeveloped Venus finger—one that is noticeably thin and stunted compared with the other fingers—can show selfishness, or a disposition tending to coldness, and a real lack of interest in aesthetics, although this may be merely a stunted response to early trauma. A good look at the heart line, Venus line, girdle of Venus, and lines of affection (see pages 81–90 and 103–108) will show if the capacity is in there somewhere.

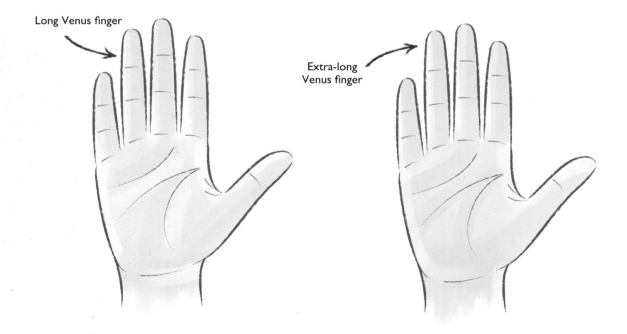

Long Venus finger

Extra-long Venus finger

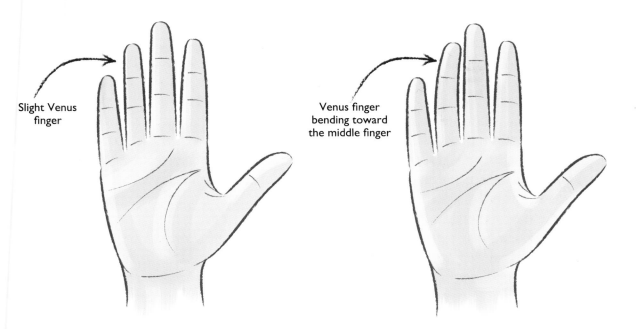

Slight Venus
finger

Venus finger
bending toward
the middle finger

A Venus finger that bends toward Saturn, the middle finger, suggests that this person needs to balance a quiet life with being engaged in the public eye; a Venus finger that bends toward Mercury, the little finger, suggests that, although this person's public life may be very public, he really wants, and needs, to keep his private life very private.

CATHERINE, DUCHESS OF CAMBRIDGE
Kate Middleton has a healthily long Venus finger and rounded fingertips, which represent her naturally warm and pleasant charisma, and her ability to be the glue that holds the family and their social world together. Her relatively short Saturn finger suggests a fairly pragmatic philosophy in life. Her fate line originates in her life line, suggesting that she is carrying on family traditions.

THE MERCURY FINGER

The little finger, also known as the pinky finger, describes how we perceive and communicate in the most private part of our lives, the most internal part of our world. It connects with our sense of honesty, trustworthiness, and trust in others. It delineates how we hear and speak. It doesn't describe our sex drive—that is indicated in the ball of the thumb and the overall musculature and padding of the hand—but it does speak of how we feel about those people with whom we are the most intimate.

A long Mercury finger—one that reaches past the top knuckle of the ring finger—suggests that sound, words, and music are important. This person picks up languages or dialects easily, and can be articulate, eloquent, and potentially manipulative with words.

A strong and substantial little finger shows someone with high emotional expectations for

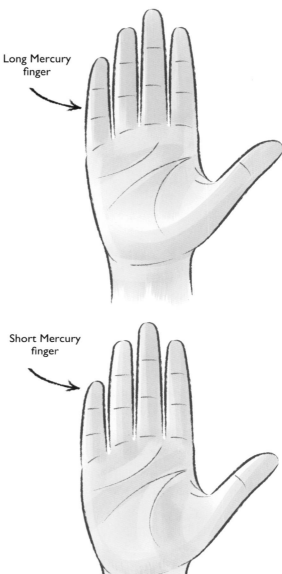

Long Mercury finger

Short Mercury finger

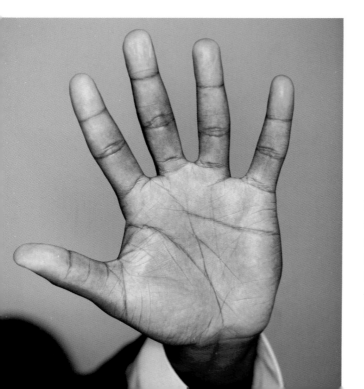

LEFT: The owner of this hand is sensitive (notice the slightly hollowed palm) with good physical vitality (a large mount of the Moon and a strong life line). He has a beautifully long little finger, denoting an ability with language and music; since his fate line originates from the life line (see page 95), these abilities were probably inherited, and put to successful professional use.

CHARLIZE THERON

Actress Charlize Theron has a well-developed Mercury finger; she is bilingual, and picks up accents with ease. She also has unusually long middle sections of the fingers, indicating a great interest in and energy spent upon her professional life.

intimate relationships. This is a person who wants to be in love with his best friend.

A short, narrow, or weak little finger can mean either tone-deafness or someone who is uncomfortable when asked to talk about his emotions, although his feelings may be very deep. Don't ask this person to tell you how he feels. Ask him to write about it or paint a picture.

Holding the little finger away from the ring finger, with a large gap in between, may indicate real problems with trust in relationships. On the non-dominant hand, this probably describes the influence of parents or other important people in this person's childhood. On the dominant hand, it describes a response to more recent relationships and how he feels about emotional intimacy at the moment.

The top of the little finger may bend sharply, or curve gently, toward the ring finger owing to a normal genetic variation, or it may catch in a door and heal with a kink. Otherwise a little finger that bends implies trouble with honesty. A crooked little finger can sometimes mean a crooked person.

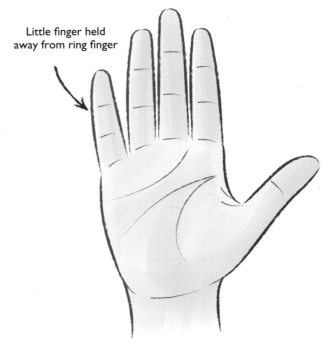

Little finger held away from ring finger

FINGER REALMS

Now let's look at each section of the finger for the next layer of information. We see the same rhythm of the three realms (see page 18) and the six shapes (see page 23) in miniature on each finger. Usually, you'll see an overall pattern of the fingers, but each finger may be slightly different. Take time to compare the lengths of the sections and look at the ends of each finger.

THE FIRST REALM (closest to the palm) tells us about our relationship to the hand's foundational realm, which is concerned with all that is earthy, manifest, pragmatic, and material, giving us our root strength.

THE SECOND REALM (middle) tells us about our relationship to the hand's middle realm—what social-professional-community environment do we create with the energy of this finger?

THE THIRD REALM (fingertips) tells us how we extend ourselves into the world—how we express ourselves, intuit, touch the world, sense and receive information. Notice the patterns on the fingertips—the whorls, arches (high and low), and loops—and look to see if there is a raised peak of sensitivity on the pad of the finger. You may need to study the fingertips through a magnifying glass. Look at the fingernails (see under the six shapes, page 55, for interpretation).

On an average hand, the sections are roughly equal. The fingertips may seem to be smaller, but if you actually measure them, you'll probably find this is not so. A balance between all three realms

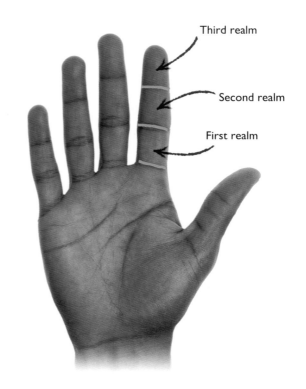

Third realm

Second realm

First realm

implies that our thinking and interaction with the world are similarly balanced around our mind, body, and spirit realms, or our mental, social-professional, and physical realms.

However, not many of us are really average. So notice, by length and width, which parts of the fingers are longer (meaning what that realm represents is particularly important to us) or shorter (meaning that part of life may not be as interesting). Notice which sections are wide (implying that we have an earthier, more muscular or indulgent approach to that part of life) and which are narrow (meaning that our approach is more aesthetic and abstracted).

PRAYING HANDS

In this classic picture of praying hands by Albrecht Dürer ("Studie zu den Händen eines Apostels," 1508), notice that the first realm of the fingers is long but thin—if you put coins between those fingers, they'd fall through the spaces. The possessor of these hands may think about the garden and worry about the practical woes of the world, but he takes a very ascetic or thoughtful approach, and he doesn't spend much time gathering material goods. This person might be able to teach business theory, but he may not be managing his own finances with any particular care.

Note the thicker, longer social-professional second realm. This is someone to whom relationships with others in a professional community are important—one reason why I suspect these hands are those of a fellow painter, or the abbot of a monastery, rather than those of a hermit mystic. The third realm appears shorter than the first two, but the nails are wide and broad, which suggests that this person wants to live out his spiritual practice and do good works in the world rather than think about it, philosophize, meditate, or otherwise live in the mind. But notice the Mercury finger on the left hand. The top section is longer than the two bottom segments and comes just above the final joint on the ring finger. Music is important to this person. He may have a love of words, work in the scriptorium, and have a real need to communicate with the people close by. There is no hair on the back of his hand, and the hands look strong and muscular but not soft or indulgent, so he might be comfortable with a celibate life, although we would have to look at the palm to be sure. On the right-hand Mercury finger (assuming this person is right-handed), the middle section is longer than it is on the other, non-dominant hand, suggesting that while he's presently comfortable communicating with coworkers, this is a developed skill, rather than an innate one.

FINGERTIPS

These fine-tune our understanding of how we express and receive information. Look at the ends of the fingers and the shape of the fingernails. There will usually be a predominance of one of the six shapes (see opposite), and this indicates a generalized way of bringing in and putting out information. The fingertips act like the nozzle on a frosting applicator—the hand contains the frosting and the pattern is expressed through the fingertips.

We use our fingertips to read braille, caress a lover, feel our work, type our thoughts. They are our antennae, our sensors, our conduits of energy and information.

Our fingernails act as a window into ourselves. A broad, wide fingernail suggests a lot of energy coming and going; a very narrow or small fingernail suggests a more focused approach or less energy exchanged with the world.

If the nails are fairly V-shaped, with the narrow end at the bottom, this suggests a wonderful physical healer, with a lot of energy pouring out into the world. But this person may not be a great listener, and may have to learn to receive.

LEFT: The young hands have a long base section of the thumb, showing strong common sense, and the fingernails are wider than they are long, meaning this person is action-oriented. The mature hands have a round fingernail on the Jupiter finger, showing that this person is generally sociable with the public, and diplomatic oblong fingernails on the Saturn and Venus fingers, indicating that she is probably a caring source of social stability for her family and community. Such smooth skin on both pairs of hands suggests that these are sensitive people, and the noticeable but not pronounced knuckles mean they both probably have a logical streak.

THE SIX SHAPES OF FINGERTIPS

Notice if one of the fingers has a different shape from the others, even slightly, because this adds significance to that finger. If a person is practical about everything except his love life, you'll see squared fingers across the board and a rounded or more pointed ring finger and/or little finger.

SQUARE FINGERTIPS show a want of clarity and common sense. Square fingertips look like sawn-off shotguns, and their owners have about as much diplomacy. They get the job done efficiently, though. Don't give them a long answer. Give them the basic facts and they'll ask what else they need to know. Notice square fingertips on engineers and mechanics who can be eloquent about their field of expertise, but give Hemingway-esque short sentences elsewhere. They are often good in the pinch and great problem-solvers.

Square fingernails are as wide as they are long, and angular, and suggest strong but specific vitality. These people have lots of energy in their fields of interest, but very little elsewhere. Those with wide but short fingernails work in bursts.

ABOVE: This person's fingernails appear wider than they are long. These solid, wide hands are those of someone who is not interested in details, but has strength and enthusiasm to offer. A round Jupiter fingernail implies a friendly, sociable manner when dealing with the public; the spatulate Saturn fingernail suggests an action-oriented personality at work, someone who wants just to do it, and is generous with his energy and time as long as you do not waste it. The middle section of his fingers appears longest of the three, which suggests that his work and standing in the community are important to him.

ROUND FINGERTIPS are the norm. Their shape implies a person who expresses himself in a friendly and socially comfortable way, with a natural sense of diplomacy and willingness to listen.

Rounded fingernails are about as wide as they are long. Large and round comes with a sturdy and durable personality. Small and round indicates people who are socially sensitive and tend to keep to themselves. They can be critical of those whose culture or habits are different from their own.

Square   Round

LEFT: These are the hands of someone who uses them to express energy in the world. The clearly spatulate fingernails act like a megaphone to expand the aperture of expression. We see them on bakers, healers, massage therapists, athletes, and adventurers—people who give generously to their world through their actions, and who can be impulsive risk-takers. Don't ask them to explain the details; ask them to show you instead.

SPATULATE OR SPLAYED FINGERTIPS are wider at the top than at the bottom of the third section. They can look like a blunderbuss, and the owners express themselves with as much enthusiasm and as little subtlety. This spatulate shape funnels or magnifies energy expressed through their hands—the massage therapist and healers who pour energy into their clients, the builders and sculptors who shape with their hands, the leaders who inspire the troops with their enthusiasm. They may have to develop listening skills. If just one or two fingers are spatulate, note the extra energy expressing from them.

Spatulate fingernails bring an instinctive enthusiasm and energy to the concerns of that finger. Those with spatulate fingernails express more than they receive, and do so through action more than words.

POINTED FINGERTIPS indicate sensitivity and perception; the more pointed, the greater the ability to pick up and produce details. The danger is stimulus overload, and these people need extra insulation in their personal life. They are often quite sensitive, even psychic, in their perceptions, and may prefer not to touch or be touched casually, as they pick up too much.

The longer and thinner the fingernail, the more the owner exists in the realm of sensibilities and less in grounded pragmatics.

Spatulate

Pointed

Oval

Rectangular

OVAL FINGERTIPS and fingernails are a variation on the round shape. The silhouette is the same, but the deeper oval fingernail suggests a person with more sensitivity and depth. It is common to have a round nail on the first finger, and deeper ovals as the fingers progress toward the little finger, implying sturdiness in public persona, but a tendency to feel and reveal more in personal and intimate life.

RECTANGULAR FINGERTIPS are a variation on square ones and have a similar interpretation.

Rectangular fingernails are squared off but deeper than they are wide. These people have a more cerebral quality than those with the square version, more interest in communication, but they still think carefully about what they say and hear. They may be slower to respond because they need to think things through. The information coming in and going out has to run the gamut of their logical mind, and they are natural skeptics.

ABOVE: These thumbs have wide and deep rectangular nails. The squared shape suggests that their owner has a basically pragmatic approach to how she receives and expresses information, while the depth of the nails suggests that she thinks carefully and likes her world to be ordered.

HEALTH ISSUES AND FINGERNAILS

If you get into conversation with someone who has markedly odd fingernails, you might want to ask if he's shared that with his doctor. Fingernails are a window into our health and circulation, and are sensitive to our overall condition.

For example, a clubbed fingernail, where the nail curves around the fingertip, may indicate lung problems or some form of inflammatory disease. Concave or spooned nails may warrant a check for iron or blood difficulties, or thyroid issues. A dented line across all the nails speaks of a time when the body received a shock, either an experience or a disease. Nails take about three to six months to grow out, which can give an approximate time for that incident.

FINGERPRINTS

The patterns or ridges of the skin on our fingertips are our unique stamp as an individual, our major identifying factor as far as the police are concerned. They help us to understand the filter system through which we work the magic of that finger, whether it is our Jupiter connection with the world at large, our Saturnine philosophy, the Venusian social-emotional creative life, or the Mercurial workings of our mind and intimate connections.

AN ARCH fingerprint shows earthiness. It's a simple pattern that flows across the fingertip like rolling prairie hills. It presents a simple, not particularly refined or convoluted, expression of this finger. The owner may have a straightforward, dependable, or serious-minded approach to the concerns of this finger, but may also have more primitive responses, some innocence or naïveté in this part of life, and have some tricky lessons to learn here.

A TENTED ARCH is a more complex or inspired arch fingerprint. It warms up the disposition, brings a note of fire, but keeps the natural simplicity and access to the primitive nature. Most true artists have a combination of refinement and a note of primitive connection, such as arches or tented-arch fingerprints on an otherwise delicate or surgical-looking hand. This adds power to the work, and those with tented arches may surprise themselves with their instinctive reactions. Time alone, and training in impulse control, may help them to direct their inner fire without getting in trouble.

A LOOP underlines the adaptability, intuition, and responsiveness of that finger. The loop flows in and out from one side of the fingertip and is associated with the rounded shape of the hand and its overtones of sociability. It's the most common fingerprint and is a comfortable one to have on Venus and Mercury fingers, because it eases personal interaction.

A DOUBLE LOOP is a complex and versatile variation. It looks like two loops interacting, each one connecting from the opposite side of the finger. Someone with a double-loop fingerprint may feel opposites meeting, or differing opinions trying to work their way through that part of life. It may give more breadth of thought but can speak of an inner tension in the expression of that finger. This person often understands both sides of the story, but may need to learn to mediate between conflicting opinions.

A WHORL has concentric circles around a still center, and resembles a target or bull's-eye. It looks self-contained, and shows eccentricity. Its owner goes his own way rather than following the herd, because he is listening to his inner muse, his own thoughts. A whorl underlies the capacity for abstract thinking and gives a certain detachment and independence to the expression of that finger.

A TEARDROP, a cross between a loop and a whorl, romantically called a peacock's eye, is an interestingly balanced fingerprint. It has the intuitive friendliness of the loop with the concentration and independence of the whorl yet without the opposing-force tension of the double loop. It's considered a mark of good fortune, because independence with intuition and charm can be a very effective combination.

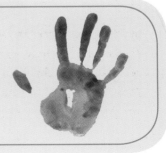

PRACTICE
Keep observing this landscape, noticing the hands of the person checking you out at the store, handing you tickets, taking your blood pressure, or stopping traffic. Get to know this terrain of our basic disposition before you go any further. It helps to look at several dozen hands before beginning to look at the roadmap of the lines.

PART II

THE ROADMAP OF THE HAND

HOW TO READ THE LINES

Now for the intimate stuff. Once in a while we get a clear view of lines on the hand of a celebrity, but usually when we're looking at the lines on a hand, we have to ask its owner's permission first! Once that is given, the person is allowing us to look into the history of her life and what direction it may take, so it is very important to remember the basic motto of all healing professions—do no harm. Do not give your sitter reason to fear the future.

If you are reading for yourself, beware the tendency of first-year medical students to feel every illness they study. If you are reading for someone who has not studied palmistry, remember that person is vulnerable. Anything said may sit in her psyche and affect her future.

This can be especially true if your sitter says she doesn't believe in palmistry. Her rational mind may reject the whole thing, but her subconscious can take it in wholesale. I remember a physicist who came to see me, and said, "I don't believe in this palmistry nonsense, but a gypsy once told me that I was going to die at 40 and I'm 39 and I don't feel so good." I reassured him that although there was a shift in his fate line and life line that suggested that he was going to calm his workaholic focus and begin to diversify his interests, I saw no sign of him dying anytime soon. His health soon began to improve.

Look for signs of hope, sources of creativity. Suggest ways to balance extremes and leave room for free will and grace to overcome the odds.

SIGNS OF CHANGE

Consider taking photographs, in good light, of your hands, or the hands of people close to you whose lives you can follow, and print them out. Alternatively, you could apply a thin coating of ink to the hand with a roller, press down hard on paper, and outline the resulting handprint with a pen. Note any major imbalances in the hands and think about suggestions for bringing life into a more harmonious relationship. Then watch the minor changes in the lines that occur after you or your friends make healthy adjustments in your daily life and in the pursuit of your goals.

FIRST IMPRESSIONS

Notice the overall pattern of lines. Do the lines dance across the hand? Are there a few simple, clear lines, or is there a light, fine network encompassing them all?

Look at the lines on the hands of people you know. Without understanding the meaning of any particular line, we can quickly notice a correlation between the overall impression of these lines and a person's disposition, how she expresses herself, and how she organizes the space around her.

Clear, rounded, soft lines correlate with round hands, friendliness, and a cozy sense of aesthetics. A fine network of soft lines is common on long, thin hands and can remind us of the way water streams over fields or fog wisps through the streets. Such lines describe a sensitive nature that absorbs its surroundings like a sponge. On these hands, not every line is significant. A soft network is evidence of a fluid and responsive soul.

Many thin but energetic lines that criss-cross the palm and look like leaping wildfire over prairie grass express the eccentric, electric, nervous energy commonly found in people with long or spatulate and muscular palms, and signal a charged, responsive, charismatic personality.

Simple, straightforward lines echo earthy, square-shaped palms and signify an organized life, and a desire to simplify, maybe oversimplify, its complexities.

But take note when the finer lines tell a different story from the one indicated by the shape of the hand. If we see a network of lines diffusing the energy along the life line of an earthy hand, or if we see strong, deep lines on a long, soft hand with delicate fingers, a hand on which we might expect to see a fine, shallow network of lines, this difference is significant.

MAJOR LINES

The arc of our life's story

Our major lines—life line, head line, heart line, and fate line—are the riverbeds, the conduits of our energy out into the world. We want to see them stronger and deeper than all the other lines, or our efforts may feel swamped and overridden. If life, head, and heart lines are equally strong and deep, that indicates a comfortable balance between body, mind, and heart. Note whether one of these major lines is underdeveloped, paler and slighter than the others, or overdeveloped and appears to overshadow or bully the other lines.

If the dominant hand has weaker lines than the non-dominant hand, then life has thrown the owner unexpected curveballs that are hard to overcome, or the choices the owner has made have not served her well so far, and her energy has become diffused and unfocused. This is common with people who drink heavily, take drugs, or respond passively to life, but can also be found on hands of people who have dealt with shattering experiences. Do not jump to judgment. Look at the non-dominant hand for potential that can be tapped into to heal and magnify the future.

If the dominant hand has stronger lines than the non-dominant hand, then the person has made healthy choices so far, which have strengthened health, heart, or mental focus. This person can congratulate herself on her work.

For those who are ambidextrous, make fewer assumptions about which hand speaks of the past and which of the future. Note the differences between the lines on each hand and talk them over with the owner to find out which feels most relevant to her future. Ambidextrous people

may show less difference between the hands, but even a fully ambidextrous person will tend to favor one hand over the other to write or to catch, and that hand will tend to show the effects of her decisions, and therefore more about her present state. If in doubt, err toward generosity, and assume that the hand with the clearest, cleanest lines speaks of her present and reflects the progress she has made so far. (For examples of dominant versus non-dominant hands, see the box on page 94 and the boxes on Barack Obama's hands on pages 77 and 93.)

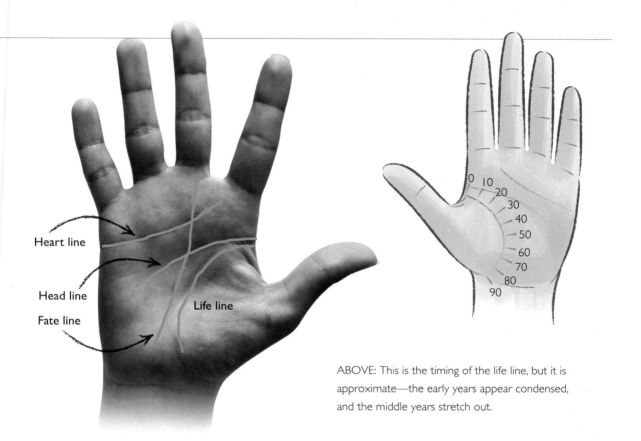

Heart line

Head line

Fate line

Life line

0 10
20
30
40
50
60
70
80
90

ABOVE: This is the timing of the life line, but it is approximate—the early years appear condensed, and the middle years stretch out.

FOUR MAJOR LINES

The head line and life line start between the thumb and forefinger and arch toward the private edge and the base of the hand. The heart line starts along the private edge under the little finger and reaches toward the forefinger, running from our most intimate place into the world. The fate line starts at the base of the palm and reaches toward the fingers. Not everybody has all these lines.

The lines should always be read in relationship to the overall pattern and shape of the hand, rather than in isolation. We read the timing of the major lines from the edge of the hand inward toward the center of the palm. This means that we can tell when things have happened. For example, an event line that crosses the life line near the start of the line (see page 69) indicates an event that happened in the early stages of someone's life.

THE LIFE LINE

Our energy meter

Most people rush to the life line first to see how long they will live. Too bad it doesn't tell us that. Many variables outside of the control of our life and habits contribute to our longevity or our quick demise. But the life line does tell us about the nature of our energy, and offers suggestions to balance and therefore sustain and increase our vitality. It also maps times of stress and times of success, loneliness, and support.

The arc of the life line defines the root of the thumb, which is the mount of the Sun, the reservoir of our vitality. The larger the arc, the stronger that person's natural physical reserves—the tanks are full, and the owner has a deep well of energy, stamina, and enthusiasm to share with the world.

The depth of the life line describes the quality of our physical vitality, the conduit of our energy out into the world. A deep life line indicates that the owner has a powerful ability to express her energy, and every opportunity to live a long and successful life. She may be impatient with lesser mortals who tire more easily, and be inclined to pour all that energy into her temperament or temper.

To balance: Some of this vitality can be worked out physically, and it would be a good idea to cultivate patience, as well as empathy with those gifted with subtler energy.

A disproportionately deep, long, arched life line, with strong coloring in the hand and a large thumb, suggests great vitality and willpower, giving the potential to be a great leader, if the heart is in the right place, or a bully.

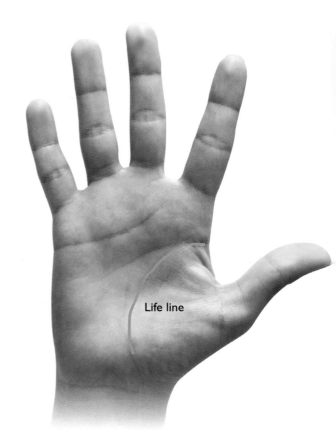

Life line

To balance: This person needs to calm down, respect the rights of others, and think out the consequences before she acts.

The narrower and closer to the thumb the life line arcs, the less energy reserves the person tends to have. If the life line is deep or the hand generally crackles with energetic lines, the owner can express a lot of energy and carry a lot of vitality, but runs more on nerves than on reserves and can run out of energy quickly.

A faint or shallow life line shows that bravery and physical vitality may be available to this person, but are not what she runs upon. She may have a lot to give but not much energy to give it with. Notice if the head line (nerves), heart line (emotions), and/or fate line (ambitions) run deep and strong instead, suggesting that these are the real motivators or sources of energy in this person's life. If the life line thins or becomes noticeably faint, this suggests a time when the person's life force thins. Look to see if it is in response to an event line, a shock to the system, or if it just thins without event, a time when energy is low and ill health could be a problem.

To balance: The quality of the conduit of the life line can be developed through exercise, good self-care, and the build-up of physical stamina.

A short life line suggests that there's not much energy for the life scheduled so far. This does not necessarily mean a short life, but a life with problems to overcome. If the hand is ruddy, the lines deep, and the life line ends abruptly, check for heart disease or circulation problems. If the life line is weak with many lines that troop off it, check for depression.

To balance: The owner needs to take responsibility for her health, and think about what would help her to find her enthusiasm and reinvest in her life.

A long life line describes the intention and energy to live a long and purposeful life. Remember, though, that events outside of our control do not necessarily show up on the life line.

A life line chained along its whole length indicates a person who was born with delicate health, and is physically sensitive to her surroundings. She may put other people's needs ahead of her own or have had difficulty in forming a clear sense of self in childhood.

To balance: Tai chi is one way to help build strength and vitality, and this, together with some confidence-building therapy, may increase the person's ability to listen to herself and uncover a sense of purpose. She needs to strengthen her health and support her digestive system to improve absorption.

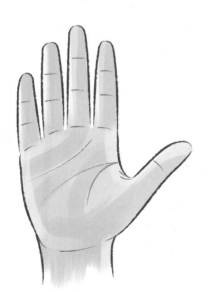

Short life line

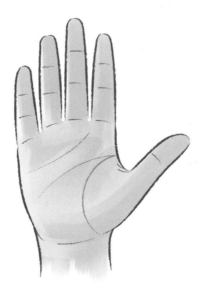

Long life line

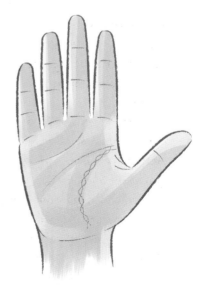

Chained life line

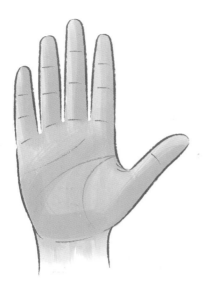

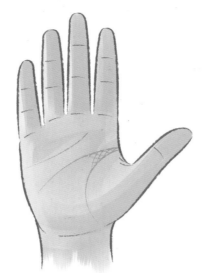

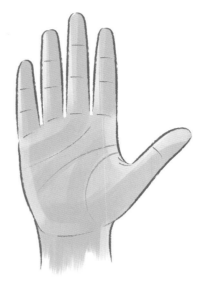

Life line and head line start together under the mount of Jupiter

Life line and head line are chained together

Life line and head line start separately

WHERE IT BEGINS

If the life line and head line start together under the mount of Jupiter, the fate and mindset of this person are well tied into her family history.

If the life line and head line originate together and stay connected for a while, it indicates that as a child, this person's mindset was formed by the family and the events going on within it.

If the life line and head line run smoothly together, this shows a normal and comfortable experience. If the life line moves smoothly out from this position, the person's early life has left her connected to her family but not feeling trapped by them.

Sometimes, the life line and head line are chained together for the first 10 years or so (see page 63). The owner may have had trouble setting boundaries with her family. She may have felt emotionally responsible for them, or have been deeply affected by the family's rhythms and stories. She may have been wrapped up in and dependent upon the family, or in full rebellion against them. Either way her sense of self was deeply but uncomfortably intertwined with the people around her, and she may have to push away from them to develop confidence and find herself. The longer the chaining goes on, the harder it has been to become an individual.

If the life line and head line start separately, this person's identity is not bound up with her family, and her independence means she may not need to push away from them. She can either stay comfortably around them, or travel the far seas to find her own path without separation pain. A sense of purpose is essential, though. Without a deep family connection to embrace or rebel against, something to aim for is necessary or she may tend to drift.

VLADIMIR PUTIN

Vladimir Putin has vitality, willpower, and an arching ambition; note the long, deep life line that arches well into the middle of the hand, a strong mount of the Sun, and a strong thumb. His Saturn line has two origins. One starts in the life line, suggesting his early work fitted with his family's ambitions; the second branch begins from the lunar mount and takes over, suggesting his secret ambitions took over in his young adult life. Note a success line branching off his life line towards the Saturn finger around his mid-thirties, suggesting that his career took a turn at this point. He has an enduring ambition, as his fate line continues up to the very top of the palm.

He has a deeply focused mentality, concentrating on a narrow range of interests, denoted by a short, deep, and clear head line. He is interested in making history, not just studying it; his head line arches slightly toward an historian's bump (a slight bulge) on the mount of Neptune. His Neptune mount is large and full, but with few lines running out of it, which suggests an active unconscious without much introspection. A large lower mount of Mars suggests that he never forgets a wrong. He has a particularly long finger of Mercury, indicating an unusually strong and persuasive ability with languages. He tends to think of the big picture rather than the details, shown by his fingers being relatively short. He is very conscious of his public image, but would rather keep a mysterious or low profile—his Jupiter finger is relatively short, although the lines in the hand focus toward that first finger.

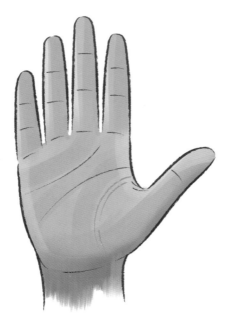

Guardian line next to life line

VARIATIONS

These suggest a life lived in chapters or segments.

GUARDIAN LINE: Also referred to as a guardian angel line or companion line, this sometimes runs like scaffolding along the side of the life line closer to the thumb. It strengthens and guards the life line, and may be there during a deeply emotional time in the owner's personal life, or when a strong friendship or romance is being forged, or when it feels as though our guardian angels are working overtime—basically, a time in our life when we feel extra support from many different sources. When the guardian angel line ends, it doesn't mean that the luck disappears, more that we have internalized the support and can now find it within. If it represents a supportive relationship, that relationship can continue but a new independence comes with it.

DOUBLE LIFE LINE: It occasionally happens that two life lines are evident, one that seems to come from the head line, the more introverted, introspective line, and a second that arches farther out into the palm, which represents the more public, extroverted side of the person's life. When these two run side-by-side comfortably, a person has an active public life and a deeply private personal life. Notice if one looks stronger and extends farther down the palm than the other. That's the side of life, either public or private, that should be encouraged.

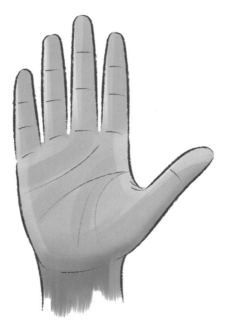

Double life line

BROKEN LIFE LINE: Sometimes the life line stops and begins again, symbolizing a major change in life path or direction, in identity, place, or health. Look to see if an event line crosses where the break occurs, indicating that it could be a reaction to an outside stimulus, such as a car accident or a promotion involving a move to Fiji. Look to see if the ends of the lines dovetail, forming a smooth transition from one phase to another, or if there's a gap before the life line starts again. A gap could show a break after an event, job loss, health problem, or other shock to the system during which the person's life shifts into limbo and appears to hold still before getting going again. Look for a guardian line for support during this time.

MODIFYING LINES

EVENT LINES: These start in the mount of the thumb, cross the life line, and extend diagonally upward. How far they go, and toward which mount, will give you a clue to the nature of the occurrence. If an event line merely crosses the life line, it is a major event of the soul, but doesn't throw the person off track. If an event line causes a dip or break in the life line, or a dip or break in the head line or heart line, an event of major proportions is indicated, one that will change the course of that person's life.

Broken life line

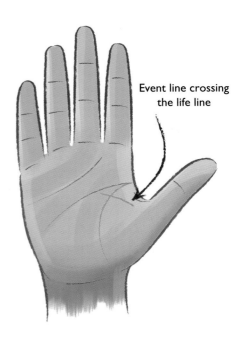

Event line crossing the life line

WORRY LINES: Thin lines, like minor event lines, radiating from the thumb toward the life line but stopping there, show concerns or times of anxiety. This can be either because events have become worrisome, or because the person is more anxious or fretful than previously.

DRAINING LINES: Small lines that originate on the life line but appear to droop downward and deplete its energy are known as draining lines. These indicate health problems, or codependent relationships, or dysfunctional life situations where the person is expending more energy than she is receiving and exhausting her reserves. Someone with a strong life line can handle these situations, but someone with a weak life line can find them severely debilitating. In any case, this person should possibly learn to hold better boundaries.

To balance: Someone with draining lines needs to create a better ecosystem for her life, so that she feels nourished by as many experiences as necessary to match the energy expended.

ISLANDS: The outline of a shape, or island, on the life line shows a time of isolation, which could be because of health or emotional circumstances. Look for an event line to begin or end the island for more information.

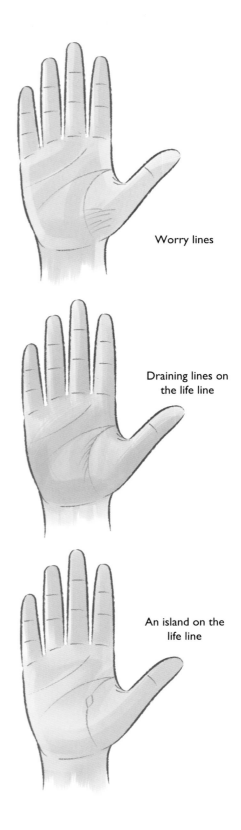

Worry lines

Draining lines on the life line

An island on the life line

AMY WINEHOUSE

Amy Winehouse, the talented musician who died at 27, probably had a quick temper—note the puffy lower mount of Mars—and a powerful musical ability, shown in her extremely long Mercury finger. She had a lot of mental and emotional energy, seen in deep head and heart lines, with limited physical reserves but generous output: a faint and narrow arc of the life line with a spatulate palm—wide at the top and narrow at the base—and a narrow, flat mount of the Sun. We can always choose to balance the pattern we see in our hand, even if it can be challenging; for a faint life line, it's important to try to build up physical strength, joy, and embodiment.

Success lines branching upward from the life line

SUCCESS LINES: These start on the life line and branch upward, as if they are suspending or supporting it, and may indicate an ambitious and idealistic disposition. Note where these lines are heading. If it is toward Jupiter, that means success in reaching out to the public; Saturn, success in work/life balance and goals accomplished; Venus, success in matters of the heart, the creative process, and popularity; Mercury, success in writing, science, or the life of the mind.

HOW IT ENDS

Where the life line stops shows a longing or calling.

If the life line wraps neatly around the base of the thumb, the person comes home in the end. She wants to live life close to her family or in a familiar place. Her philosophical mindset remains close to her origins.

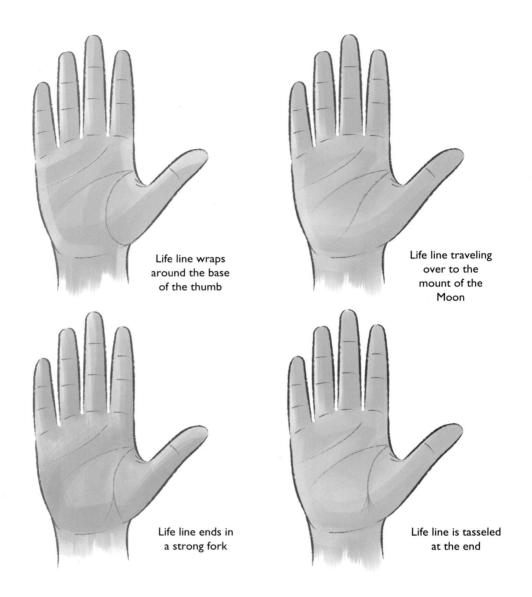

Life line wraps around the base of the thumb

Life line traveling over to the mount of the Moon

Life line ends in a strong fork

Life line is tasseled at the end

If the life line travels over to the mount of the Moon, away from the thumb, that person has a soul wanderlust and wants to travel to a faraway country or to a philosophical mindset very different from the one with which she was born.

If the life line ends in a strong fork, versatility of the mind is indicated, shown in both independence and the ability to stay connected to family roots. It usually signifies a healthy and engaged old age.

If the life line is tasseled at the end, the life force may feel fragmented or diffuse from ill health, uncertainty, or fading thinking.

To balance: Meditation and staying physically active can help, and good long-term health insurance is reassuring.

THE HEAD LINE

Our mind's altimeter

The head line describes the nature and direction of our thinking process. It begins where the story of our psyche begins, connected to our childhood at the root of our life line, and is found between thumb and forefinger. The length of the head line does not show how intelligent we are but the breadth of our interests. Its arc and depth describe the power and attitude of the mind.

A deep, strong, clear head line shows a very strong-minded person who can stay on track no matter the obstacles, concentrate for long periods, and see a project through to completion. Often, a head line deepens and strengthens as time goes by and the person develops her individuality and finds a sense of purpose.

A straight and level head line shows a levelheaded person, who is keen on common sense and logical evidence, and less interested in theory or exploring alternatives. This person will be interested in science, a structured and practical profession, or one that follows a time-honored tradition.

The shorter the head line, the more focused and narrow the interest. A deep, short head line may belong to someone who has a strong mind and a specific interest. A shallow or chained short head line may belong to someone who has trouble with concentration or mental strength. A truly short head line may indicate trouble with empathy and understanding another person's perspective.

To balance: Interests should be stretched to create more common ground with beloveds.

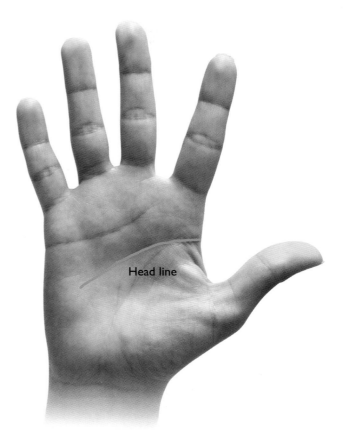

Head line

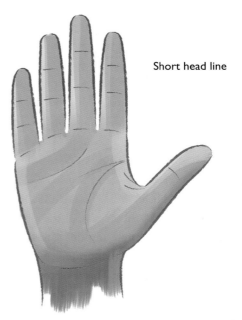

Short head line

Head line travels toward
the mount of the Moon

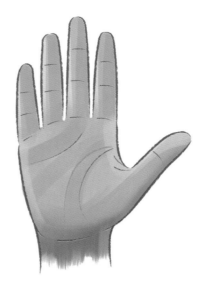

Head line travels down toward
the mount of Neptune

Head line wraps around
the side of the hand

The longer the head line, the broader the person's interests. The farther the head line dives into the heel of the hand, the richer the connection to imagination and subconscious. A head line that arcs gracefully toward the mount of the Moon describes an active mind with a compassionate and/or creative bent. Appeal to this person's curiosity with a fresh approach or creative angle.

If the head line appears to droop down into the mount of Neptune, the mind touches into the dream world, intuition, and compassionate imagination, but this person can be prone to depression or get lost in inner worlds.

An extended head line—one that is long enough to wrap around the side of the hand—shows a most active mind, but this can stray into an overactive or hypervigilant mind, which can lead to nervous problems. This is of concern if the heart and life lines also appear drained (see page 70).

To balance: Exercise and developing physical strength can help to create a more rounded life, as can building skills to express creativity, meditating, and trying to find some philosophical or spiritual perspective. The answer to these mental problems cannot be found just by analyzing the mind (although therapy can help), but through moving toward a life balanced between mind, body, and spirit. This also applies to balancing a drooping head line.

A faint or shallow head line shows someone easily tossed on the winds of emotion and other people's opinion, or shaken up by events.

To balance: A person can strengthen the head line by intensely pursuing an interest she loves, something that builds concentration, whether it's a sport, an art form, or mental activity.

A chained head line shows a nervous disposition, someone who has trouble concentrating or knowing her own mind in the face of stronger wills. This person may be psychically sensitive, more aware of other people's needs than of her own. She may have been trained into this as a child by having to adapt to strong personalities in the family.

To balance: The owner needs to develop healthy boundaries with people close to her. She has to learn to hear herself first and loudest, then become aware of what other people need and think, and find a balance between them.

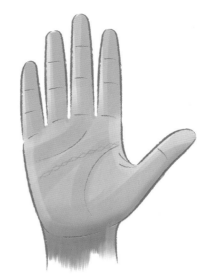

Chained head line

VENUS WILLIAMS

Superb athlete Venus Williams has a wonderfully square hand, slightly rounded at the bottom, which implies that she has abundant physical energy and a great ability to respond, as well as a fundamentally pragmatic but friendly nature that expresses itself in a clear, levelheaded, practical way. Note the deep, clear, but short head line, indicating that she has great focus on her specific interests. She is open, having a rounded upper palm and rounded fingertips, but not easy to get to know—her heart line appears to stop under her Saturn finger. Her life and head lines are connected for a long stretch, which suggests that her family has provided most of her emotional context well into her adult years.

WHERE IT BEGINS

See pages 66 and 86 for connections between head, heart, and life lines. Someone with a head line that begins separately from the life line has a deep inner world, confidence in her own opinion, or a karmic journey very different from her family's. One that starts on the mount of Jupiter indicates an ambitious, extroverted person, with a public-oriented mentality.

HOW IT ENDS

A head line that ends in a fork is often called the writer's or the lawyer's head line because it indicates an ability to see logically and concretely, as well as creatively and sympathetically. If the fork is deep, the person may have a real gift for seeing both sides but feel an uncomfortable pull between pragmatic logic and narrow idealism.

A head line that runs straight and then arches up toward the mount of Mercury shows an ability to disconnect from the emotions. This person may be considered cold or lost in her studies, or have trouble integrating head and heart. This type of head line may be found on people who bury themselves in business or research.

MODIFYING LINES

THINNING PATCH: If the head line grows light or thin, this person experienced a time when it was hard to cope. Look for signs of drug or alcohol use, or a need to retreat from the world and not push on with life.

ISLANDS: An outline shape, or island, on the head line shows a time of loneliness, when the person felt unsupported or isolated by the people around her, and so had to go it alone. Look for an event line (see page 69) to begin or end the island for more information.

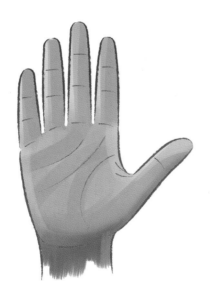

Head line starts
separately from life line

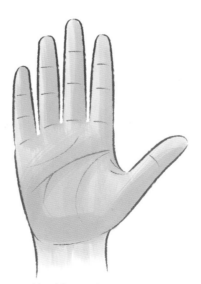

Head line ends in
a fork

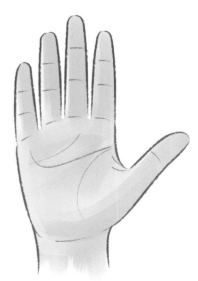

Head line travels up
toward the mount of
Mercury

BARACK OBAMA—LEFT HAND

President Obama has a deeply forked head line on his left hand (his dominant, active hand), with one branch showing imagination and sensitivity, and a shorter one showing levelheaded concentration. The life and head lines start together but separate quickly, and the relatively low-energy life line launches into a path far from his family's origins. The fate line runs deep and true and shows determination. Also notice a strong heart line that reaches up to the edge of the palm between the Jupiter and Saturn fingers, a position known for supporting a healthy and happy chosen family life.

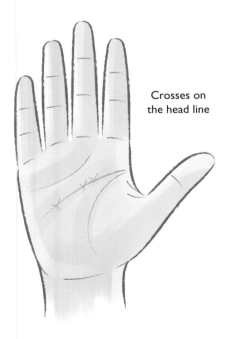

Crosses on the head line

DRAINING LINES: Small lines that originate on the head line but appear to droop downward and drain its energy indicate times of worry, depression, or mental exhaustion.

CROSSES: Either freestanding or formed by an event line crossing the life line and the head line, crosses indicate tough decisions or crises that have tested the owner's judgment and challenged her to stretch her mind.

SUCCESS LINES: Lines that start on the head line and branch upward tell of uplifting moments, either successes that improve confidence, or spiritual or philosophical understandings that lift the mind. Notice the mount toward which the lines reach.

NELSON MANDELA

Nelson Mandela's hand shows a wide and well-balanced great quadrangle. Notice the life line and head line running together smoothly in the early years, and the head and heart line running evenly parallel. The thinning patch on the life line indicates his years of internment. The head line leaps away from the life line and is relatively short and clear, suggesting that he focused deeply on what mattered to him. The relatively short Saturn middle finger suggests that, although he was thoughtful, it was not good enough for him to philosophize; he needed to act on that philosophy. Lots of room above the heart line suggests a big heart and a wide-ranging mind even though he concentrated on his interests. Notice that the top sections of his fingers are the longest, showing a deeply idealistic person. Also notice that the head line points to an historian's bump, a slight bulge on the outer edge of the hand about halfway up the lunar mount that shows a deep interest in recent history. He helped make it happen.

THE GREAT QUADRANGLE

The plain between the head and heart line is referred to as the great quadrangle.

If there is a smooth, wide area between the head and heart line, this person will have common sense. She will be able to make emotional decisions with her heart and mental decisions with her head, and make sure the two work together naturally.

If there is a very narrow band between head and heart line, the person may not have much interior bandwidth for differences of opinion or ways of life. This is someone who can be narrow-minded, or very shy. In either case, this person is self-protective, and may choose not to take risks.

Tiny lines weaving between the head and heart lines show someone who may think with her heart and feel with her head. Notice if one of the lines seems stronger or more dominant than the other, indicating if the person is more heart or more head oriented.

A clear, independent cross in the great quadrangle, beneath the mount of Saturn, and not involving the fate line or event lines crossing the area, is known as a mystic cross. It shows that the head and the heart are connected in a way that bestows intuition and a potential interest in the occult or in mystical experiences.

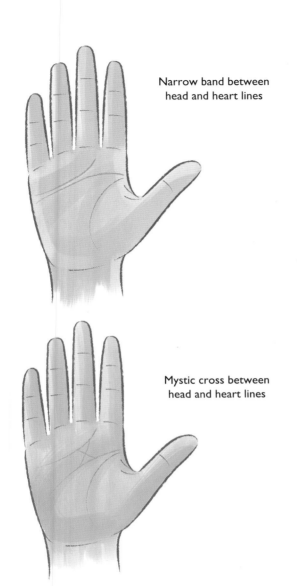

Narrow band between
head and heart lines

Mystic cross between
head and heart lines

ABOVE: This person took a step of independence in her late teens or early adulthood—the head line breaks away from the life line. She is interested in foreign cultures, and may travel or move far from where she was born—her life line doesn't wrap around the base of the thumb, but goes toward the mount of the Moon. She has the healthy, wide and even quadrangle of a person able to balance head and heart to make healthy decisions.

PALMAR CREASE

Sometimes, there is no great quadrangle because the head and heart line have merged into a single palmar crease (known in most palmistry systems as a simian line, but I prefer this medical term). Look to see if the head line is dominant and has incorporated the heart line, almost as if it ate it up, or if the heart line is dominant. The dominant line will tend to override the consumed line.

A single palmar crease gives its owner the ability to focus absolutely, even obsess. It is found on the hands of those who possess ingenious scientific or engineering minds, inventors, musicians, people who throw themselves into a line of work and whose personal life might suffer because of it, or people who throw themselves into their work to avoid messy emotions. A small percentage of people with a single palmar crease may be diagnosed on the Asperger's autism scale or have some other neurological difference.

In a partial palmar crease, the head and heart lines start to merge, but one line branches in the normal direction. This describes a milder version of the single crease. Someone with a partial palmar crease may well be able to develop both her emotional and her mental life, with care.
To balance: Healthy emotional relationships should be consciously developed. If this is a stretch, counseling or coaching may be necessary. Spiritual or philosophical pursuits are a way to engage the heart and higher mind.

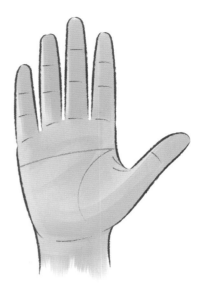

Single palmar crease

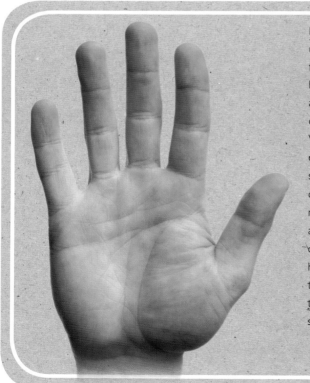

People with a single palmar crease often have unusual abilities to concentrate on their chosen field of interest, even obsess about it. Here the head line subsumes most of the heart line, creating a single line across the palm with a fragment of heart line above. This becomes a girdle of Venus (see page 105), which implies a need for emotional stimulation, but this person may miss some ordinary social cues and have problems creating rich and steady relationships. As a child, his mental condition was very connected to the ups and downs of family life (life line and head line are chained together for the first inch), and he tends to hold on to wrongs and resentments (indicated by the large lower mount of Mars), which contributes to his emotional wariness. For more about the shape of this hand, see page 36.

THE HEART LINE

Emotional capacity and stories that build the heart

Our emotional lives are complex, and not defined by one line. We can't look at a hand and tell from the lines if its owner will be happily married to a black-haired stranger by the age of 36. But reading the hand can help you to know what to do with your one wild and precious heart, and maximize the potential for comfortable and easy relationships.

To get a picture of a person's complicated emotional life through a combination of components in the hand, concentrate first on the overall texture of the hand as a clue to sensuality, comfort, and willingness to make an effort. Then check out the heart line for emotional history and capacity. Fine-tune this impression by looking for a girdle of Venus for emotional excitability, and lines of affection on the side of the hand for interest in forming long-term bonds (see the next section on minor lines for more information on the girdle of Venus and lines of affection).

The heart line starts underneath the little finger, on the intimate side of the hand, arcs across the hand, and usually ends somewhere between the mount of Saturn and the mount of Jupiter or dives back into the life line. It describes how comfortable we are meeting new people and making new friends, our sensitivities, our romantic history, and what stirs our heart. The heart line maps how we relate to people, life experience, and our soul's passions, and so describes how we extend ourselves in relationships as well as in business and finance.

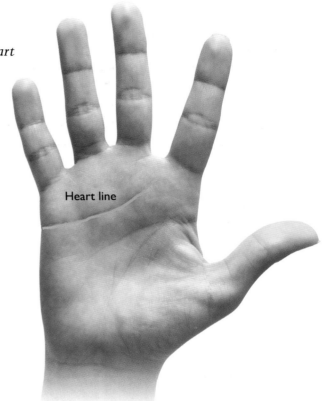

Heart line

When we look at the heart line of a potential romantic interest, we can find clues about what makes that person comfortable to love. If it comes to it, he may choose to stretch himself beyond his comfort zone, but it's not a good idea to push him out there. He may not be able to sustain that different condition until he has grown into it on his own.

More than other lines, the heart line shows choices we've made to feel safe. If someone is a guarded soul, we can invite him out of his shell, but we shouldn't dismantle his defenses and insist he loves unless we know for sure that he will be there for the rest of his life. Don't ask a person with a pale, thin heart line to run away and have an affair in Borneo. Even if he does go, he'll feel scared and dependent. Don't ask a person with a short, stubby heart line to donate money to children in a faraway country, but do ask him to help rebuild the old lady's house down the street. These people need to see the connection. And don't ask a person with a deep, strong, heart line that arches up into the Saturn finger to be polyamorous, or a person with a wired, forked heart line to be monogamous after the first date. Instead, play to their natural aptitudes, and possibly help them stretch one step beyond.

DEPTH AND QUALITY OF THE HEART LINE

A strong, deep heart line indicates an emotionally passionate person. On a quiet hand, you might say still waters run deep. On an active hand, feel that deep heart line pour emotional charisma into the world. These are people who love and hate intensely. Someone with a heart line deeper and stronger than head or life line will be run by passions, and will make radical emotional decisions. Elsewhere on the hand, look for attributes of willfulness that would exacerbate this passion, or signs of patience that would ameliorate it.

This kind of heart line is usually a sign of people who know the worth of material goods and look after the people, work, and things they value; they may not want to let them go. They can be successful and fair business people in a field they honestly care about.

To balance: Cultivating compassion is good for someone with a disproportionally deep or wide heart line, perhaps by working for a good cause, while at the same time appreciating and developing common sense. When the heart is feeling unusually turbulent, a radical act of kindness or creativity can take up all that extra heart energy.

A heart line that is shallow and pale compared with the other major lines points to a person who doesn't have much emotional energy, is uncertain about her feelings, and may be afraid to invest in herself. A shallow heart line can also be a sign of circulation or heart issues, either physical or metaphorical. This is someone who may be ruled more by mind and nerves than by heart, or, owing to some early problems in the family, she may choose not to take emotional risk. These people may appreciate beautiful things around them, but a certain detachment gives them an abstracted business sense—they may be interested in being successful by pursuing their particular talent or by cultivating the process of business, but not because they're passionate about it. If the heart line becomes shallow for a brief section only, this refers to an emotionally or physically exhausting time in the person's life.

To balance: Finding safe and supported ways to use the heart is good for a person with a weak or shallow heart line. The bullies of the past should not be allowed to stunt the future. Therapy may help untangle early emotional restraints placed upon the person by childhood events, but then it helps to have safe places to love. She could volunteer at the dog pound or help out at a children's nursery. She could practice heart-centered metta meditation, and meditate on loving all sentient beings. Suggest she gets a pet, a cause, a place to exercise the heart without feeling too personally exposed until the heart feels stronger and more ready to extend.

An unusually high heart line that cuts into the fingers' mounts can mean a very guarded heart, someone not interested in extending herself emotionally unless she feels very safe. Any form of underdeveloped heart line, whether thin, pale, high, or short, is a sign of someone who may be a kind person, with religious or philosophical scruples against meanness, but who has the capacity to detach and not empathize with the people whose lives she crosses. If found with other signs of a strong mind and a materialistic nature, a high heart line can point to someone who is ruthless in business.

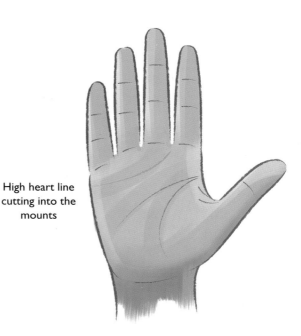

High heart line cutting into the mounts

A short heart line is a sign of someone who does not extend herself emotionally. She may appear emotionally stingy, coldhearted, unable to empathize. She will tend to be conservative in all things, or may sublimate emotional needs into more material needs if the rest of the hand looks cushy and self-indulgent. A more benign possibility is that she has chosen to protect her heart in this lifetime because of early emotional disappointments or trauma from another life. These people may respond very well if another person reaches out to them and proves trustworthy, but they are still unlikely to take emotional risks. Look for a girdle of Venus (see page 105) or a strong, curved, open-minded head line to buffer the effects of a short heart line.

To balance: Someone with a tight, short, or shallow heart line should consciously try to build empathy by learning to love when it feels safe to love—caring for a goldfish or a cat, volunteering at a homeless shelter, working for a good cause that allows the heart to engage with the world without taking personal emotional risks, until it feels ready to do so.

Short heart line

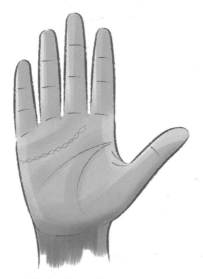

Chained heart line

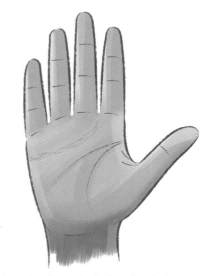

Heart line formed of a bundle of wires

A chained heart line shows an emotionally changeable or labile personality, and is often found on a hand that has a fine network of little lines across the palm. These people may be unusually sensitive and responsive; their feelings are strong but change quickly. They can also be so emotionally empathetic that they are more aware of how everyone around them feels than of how they feel themselves. This sensitivity can trigger social anxiety, or let them be controlled by the ones they love, unless they have a strong thumb, a sign of solid willpower. These sensitive folk can be easily hurt when they argue with beloveds. It may be hard for them to find words for how they feel, although they can readily express their feelings in poetry, art, and action.

Most people have some chaining at the beginning of their heart line, as a certain amount of emotional volatility is natural through childhood and adolescence. If the line is briefly chained, this sensitive volatility didn't go on

forever. If the chaining reaches all the way across, these people have learned to extend themselves in relationships in spite of this sensitivity. If the chained heart line stops short, they may have chosen to protect their heart by not emotionally overextending themselves. However it is, trust their choice.

A heart line that appears to be a bundle of wires is a sign of a wired emotional life. These people may feel volatile in relationships, and have many different friendships or loves that act like outriggers so no one relationship can take them down. Highly responsive, they are no one's Rock of Gibraltar, but can flirt with the best of them and inspire the troops with their enthusiasm.

Both the chained and the wiry heart line are common in those with artistic personalities—warm, sensitive people, reactive to those around them, with a potentially volatile temperament and a creative approach that reflects thinking

ANGELINA JOLIE

Left-handed Angelina Jolie has deep feelings with a practical and rational foundation—shown by her long rectangular palm—and strong willpower. She is also extremely independent, as shown by her unusually large and low-set thumb. Note the large lower section of thumb, the knotty lower knuckles, and the extra space above the head–heart axis—she has common sense and an intelligent, philosophical mind with a logical slant. This helps with her sensitive nature—seen in her hollow palm. Her fingers are long and narrow—she may have money, but that is not what motivates her. She holds her little finger apart, suggesting early trust issues with members of the opposite sex, and since it's on her dominant hand, this may still affect her interactions. Her lines are faint, covered with a network of fine lines, meaning that she runs more on nerves than she does on physical vitality, and needs time alone to regroup. Her disposition is open-minded and open-hearted (there's a broad space between her head and heart lines), but her emotional life has perhaps not been easy; an early sense of isolation has built in self-sufficiency and it may take her a while to trust people—her heart line appears chained in the early years and stops under her Saturn finger with faint branches going toward the far side of the hand, the Jupiter finger, and the space between her Jupiter and her Saturn fingers. She is energized by her connection to the public and her philanthropic efforts (the heart line branches to the far side of the hand and toward Jupiter), but once she makes a personal connection, she can be very private and possessive with her beloveds—notice the branch that runs between Jupiter and Saturn.

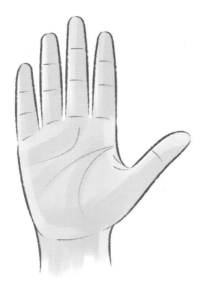

Heart line curving toward
mount of Saturn

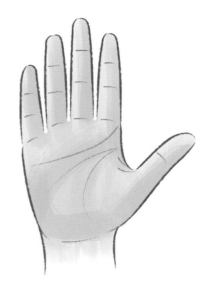

Heart line curving
toward Jupiter

outside the box. The chained heart line points to someone who cares very much about other people's opinions, even painfully so. The wiry heart line person is aware of these opinions but more impervious to them because of a fiery nature—someone more likely to be a gourmand than gourmet of love affairs.

To balance: Chained and wiry heart line people need to learn to trust themselves to care for and protect their heart, and to love themselves as much as they love others. They need to come to value trusted friendships. The love of a steady friend or a good dog can add stability, and this can spread to the rest of their relationships.

WHERE IT BEGINS

Observe the beginning of the heart line under the little finger. It usually mirrors the quality of the early years on the head and life lines. Emotionally

volatile chaining or small disappointment lines from childhood and adolescence are normal, but look for unexpected breaks, blocking lines, or major disappointment lines. Check for timing and more information on the life line.

THE ARC OF THE HEART LINE

A graceful arc that runs parallel with, but not too close to, the head line and leaves room above for substantial mounts under the fingers shows generosity and a healthy emotional capacity.

The closer in the heart line curves, reaching toward the mount of Saturn or Jupiter, the more private, intimate, possessive, and potentially untrusting the person will tend to be.

The farther the heart line reaches out toward the public edge of the hand and toward the mount of Jupiter or beyond, the more outgoing, extroverted, altruistic, and collective is the heart;

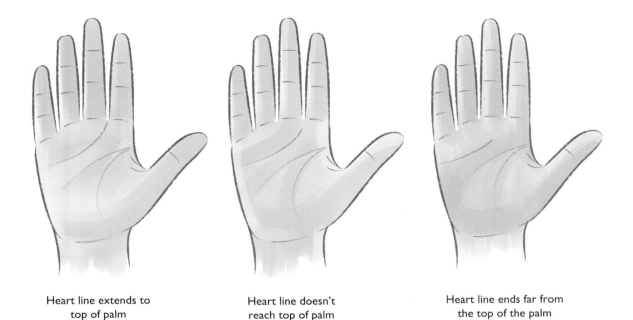

Heart line extends to
top of palm

Heart line doesn't
reach top of palm

Heart line ends far from
the top of the palm

these are people who know what the crowd needs, but may forget their beloved's birthday.

HEART LINE EXTENSION

The heart line is a line of relationship, and relationship requires that we extend ourselves. Note how far the heart line extends and what mount it reaches toward.

If the heart line extends to the top edge of the palm, this is someone who is willing to make the first move toward friendship or group interaction.

If the heart line doesn't quite reach the edge, or just its hair lines make it, this is someone who may be open to new friendships but requires the other person to take that first step and show true interest. Despite a natural sense of reserve, she may be comfortable as a public figure, although having few close private friends. Generally, this person responds well to an overture.

If the heart line ends a long way from the palm's top edge, the person may have an inner lava flow of warmth, but will be shy and hesitant to connect. Other people will have to instigate the friendship, prove that they're really interested, and keep proving that they care, in order to access that warmth.

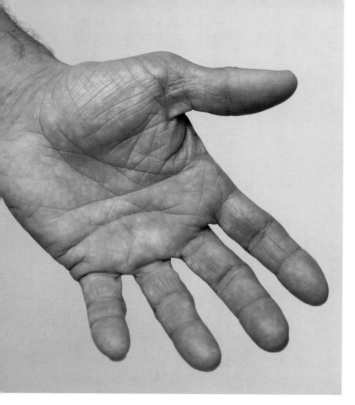

ABOVE: The heart line reaches toward the space between Jupiter and Saturn, the family man position. This man is a caring person. He may be open to new friendships but will probably not reach out—the heart line doesn't quite reach the edge of the palm. But if another person extends himself and proves trustworthy, he will be a good friend—see how another line starts at the edge and reaches toward the heart line, with a small gap between. An event line cuts across from early childhood on the life line to this gap, and a drooping line from the heart line curves toward an island of isolation on the life line—some things that happened when he was young, and again in his adolescence, have discouraged his heart. He needs proof that it's safe to care; he may be possessive in relationships, but he can care deeply, seen in the strong line of affection on the mount of Mercury. Sensuality is important to him—the heart line is strong, the wide palm is curved at the top, and he has full mounts of the Sun and Mars.

WHERE THE HEART LINE ENDS
The goals of relationship
(See illustration opposite)

A: A heart line that reaches toward Saturn is a sign of people who have an emotional prime directive to be safe. They may have an active private emotional life, but need trust to blossom. They will tend to take things personally, and can be passionate but possessive or territorial about their love, protective of their own interests and the interests of the people they are closest to. If their feelings are hurt, they can get mean or withhold their warmth as a way of controlling the situation.

B: A heart line that reaches between Saturn and Jupiter can be thought of as the family line. This shows a comfortable balance between personal and community life, introversion and extroversion. If the line reaches to the edge of the palm, this person values the intimacy, generosity, and loyalty that supports a comfortable family life.

C: A heart line that reaches toward Jupiter indicates people with idealistic views of relationships, who have high expectations. They want to live by their philosophy, and need a spiritual connection with their beloved, receiving a lot of emotional charge out of their community or groups. They may feel passionately connected within, but can seem a little abstract or righteous to their companions. Altruistic, they kindly dive in to help others when they see a problem, but may have to realize that they do not always have the best answer. To stretch their soul, they need to learn to listen to and honor other people's worldview.

D: A heart line that reaches toward the public side of the hand, landing between the head line and the Jupiter finger, is indicative of those who can connect to the public but may not have the foggiest idea how to relate to people in intimate situations. They may be very lovable but they need to learn to see those closest to them. It's not that they mean to be cold or inconsiderate, but their antennae are just calibrated farther afield. They may be loners or prefer communal love, such as in an ashram or monastery, or get their emotional charge from helping disaster victims or other altruistic callings; or they may be cold fish. They may love humankind or global business, it's just people they can't stand. Look at the rest of the hand for signs of warmth and engagement, or signs of calculated materialism.

E: If the heart line dives back across the life line the owner experienced a great emotional disappointment that left the heart daunted— the disappointed optimist, the heartbroken child, the person whose first love betrayed her. If this line begins an island on either the heart or the life line, the owner felt isolated in response. If it occurs with a broken heart line, the disappointment changed the course of her life. If after this connection with the heart line, the life line actually strengthens or the fate line bolts ahead, she threw herself into work. If the whole heart line dives down, this experience changed the nature of her love life forever, although she can learn to trust again. If it is merely a branch of the heart line and the heart line continues on its merry way, then that disappointment may be a deeply woven part of her story, but it did not interrupt her capacity to love.

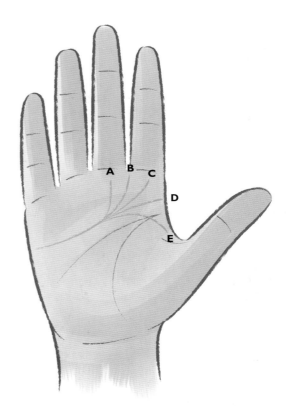

Where the heart line ends

VARIATIONS ON THE HEART LINE

A: If the heart line ends in a fork, the person is emotionally versatile, having a personal side to her life, and a more public edge. Look under "Where the heart line ends" on page 88 to read about the significance of each fork. If that fork has so many branches that it looks like a tassel, the person may be emotionally diffuse and have trouble settling into one direction, one relationship, or one cause in life.

B: A broken heart line can signify a broken heart or a time when the heart was deeply tested. If it is a small, dovetailed break, the person recovered easily. If there is a gap in the line, the shock put her emotional life on hold for some time. For more information, look for either fine lines going from the break to the life line, or for an echoing disturbance on the life line, such as a break, a drooping line, or an island. Use the markings on the life line to gauge the approximate timing of the events.

C: Draining lines are small lines that originate on the heart line but appear to droop downward and drain its energy. If there are just a few downward lines, they tell of sadness, loss, or disappointment. If they are consistent down the length of the heart line, they indicate either a tendency to get into codependent relationships in which more is given than received, or a propensity to see the best in others, miss clues, and often be disappointed.

To balance: People with draining lines should try to develop a more lovingly realistic view of those around them, and celebrate when they achieve this aim.

D: Islands on the heart line show a time of social isolation. People who have these islands went through a time when they felt disconnected

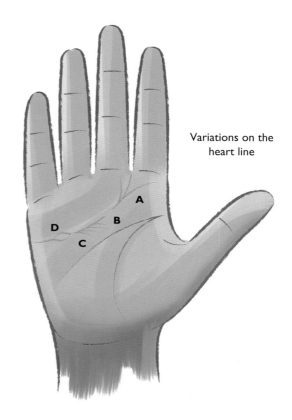

Variations on the heart line

from those around them. They may have changed schools or countries, or a beloved may have died, and they were unable to share their feelings. Perhaps their heart was broken, or maybe they were teased and felt like an outcast. Event lines on the other major lines will provide clues to what happened and how long it took.

If the island occurs earlier than the person's present age, she has found ways to reconnect. Let this be a discussion. If she does not remember any time of isolation, and the island appears to be at an age older than she is now, she needs to take care of her connections, particularly under times of stress. Solitude is lovely, isolation is not.

THE FATE LINE
Energy, ambition, focus

The fate line runs from the wrist toward the fingers, but not everybody has one. Let's define fate. We are not talking about our wyrd—a concept of irresistible, inevitable, personal destiny. Instead, the fate line describes how much energy we put into working our fate, how much ambition, willfulness, determination, and focus we bring to improving our lot in life.

A person can strive to improve by studying, and working hard, but still not be successful as far as the world is concerned. He will have a strong fate line. Another person can be very successful in the family business just by putting in the expected good day's work but not be ambitious for more. He will have no particular fate line.

The person described as a self-made millionaire, politician, or somebody who finds his way in the world, beating new paths, will always have a strong fate line, because he has made the effort to push forward.

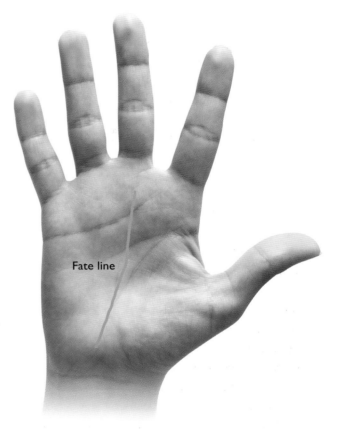

Fate line

These muscular hands with strong thumbs, straight fingers and a clear, deep, and long fate line on the left hand belong to someone with strength of mind, body, and will, who has lived with great determination and by his own principles. He is philosophic and professional rather than personal (note the clear lines and long middle finger sections); to work with him, appeal to his clear goals.

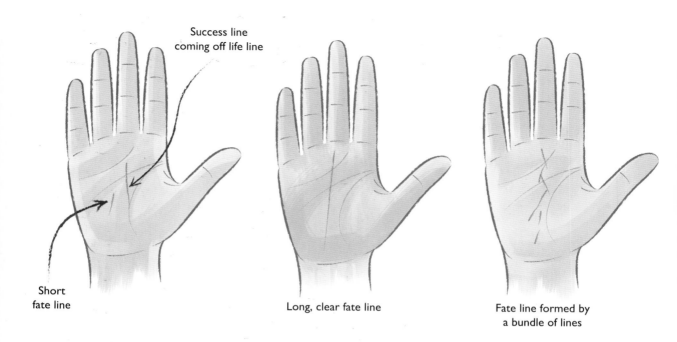

Success line
coming off life line

Short
fate line

Long, clear fate line

Fate line formed by
a bundle of lines

DEPTH AND LENGTH

These attributes of the fate line describe the strength and consistency of the ambitious effort a person puts into his fate.

On a clear, clean, practical, earth hand with few lines, we may observe a short fate line in the middle of the hand and a success line coming off the life line. This person probably settled comfortably into a practical routine early on, but then decided to start his own business, double the size of the family farm, or invent something he could take to market. He has spent most of his life generally content, but threw himself into an ambitious spurt in the middle years.

A long, straight, clear fate line that runs the length of the hand is a sign of clear goals and consistent effort. This is a person with ambition backed up with sweat equity, attributes that usually bring success. But to understand what kind of success, we must look at the values of the rest of the hand. Success for one person may

be a quiet life spent perfecting a unique skill; for another person it may mean becoming a world leader.

Hands that are naturally covered with a network of fine lines often have a bundled fate line composed of different pieces stacked together. The path of these people's careers may jump around, because they experiment to find themselves, they choose to gather skills from different directions, or they get restless and reinvent themselves regularly. That may be just the way they like it—these hands with busy lines belong to people who hate to be bored. If the rest of the lines look strong and deep, they enjoyed this reinvention. If the breaks are connected to worry lines, or the other major lines look tentative or unsettled, this constant reinvention may have been an uncomfortable response to difficult experiences, loss of interest, or minor failures. But as long as the fate line continues, they try to make it work.

BARACK OBAMA—RIGHT HAND

President Obama's right (non-dominant) hand shows a clear fate line,
starting on the mount of Neptune and heading straight up from the wrist.
This is someone who can combine dreams and practicality and, with
inspired pragmatism, make it so.

A missing fate line just means lack of effort.
Now, people can lack the will to put in the effort
for change because they are perfectly content
with their life as it is. Whether they have a trust
fund, or run the family farm, or wander the globe
following endless summer, they choose not to put
energy into changing their lot in life. This goes
for both everyday routine and the overarching

pattern of life. They may tend to wander in the
middle of a project, procrastinate, get distracted
by a good conversation, or be easily discouraged
by obstacles.

If there is a fate line on the passive hand
but not on the dominant hand, something may
have caused this person to give up—look for
problems, such as tough event lines, a chained

early life line, and tangled family responsibilities, or a weakening of the life line, implying a time of lower vitality for a possible cause. Alternatively, he has not yet found his passion, something that will excite him enough to put in the effort.

If someone has no fate line on the passive hand but a strong one on his active hand, he has striven to improve his lot in life, found unexpected resources, and is making an effort past anybody's expectations.

Be careful not to judge someone by the condition of his fate line. For some people, a lifetime of contentment, even of survival, marks a huge growth in their souls. Honor their choices.

To balance: It helps people with a missing fate line to have checklists and practical short-term goals so they can stay on track.

If a fate line comes up from the wrist but ends at an event line that crosses the life line, that person may have begun a career, encouraged by family, and continued successfully until an event ended that period of his life. If the fate line stops there, he abandoned his efforts to be ambitious. If after a break the fate line picks up again closer to the fingers, he has found new inspiration and re-engaged with fresh ambition.

If a person has multiple fate lines, many threads of his life matter to him. Someone who

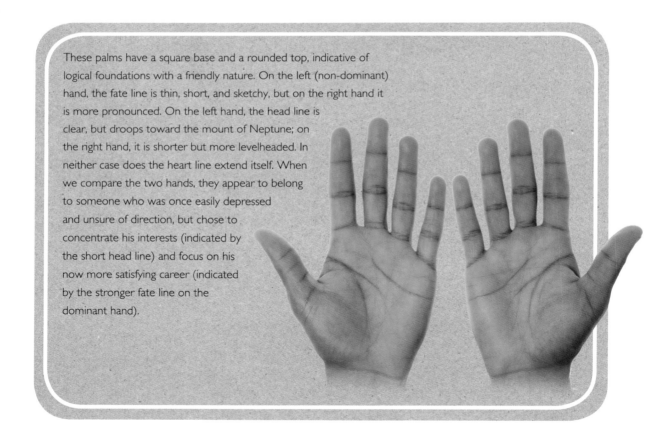

These palms have a square base and a rounded top, indicative of logical foundations with a friendly nature. On the left (non-dominant) hand, the fate line is thin, short, and sketchy, but on the right hand it is more pronounced. On the left hand, the head line is clear, but droops toward the mount of Neptune; on the right hand, it is shorter but more levelheaded. In neither case does the heart line extend itself. When we compare the two hands, they appear to belong to someone who was once easily depressed and unsure of direction, but chose to concentrate his interests (indicated by the short head line) and focus on his now more satisfying career (indicated by the stronger fate line on the dominant hand).

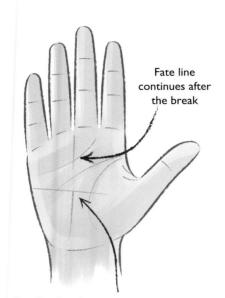

Fate line
continues after
the break

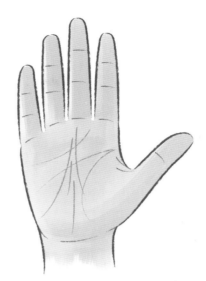

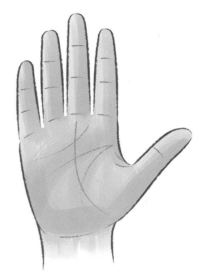

Fate line breaks at an event
line that crosses the life line

Multiple fate lines

Fate line originates
from the mount of
the Sun

is a successful project manager at the bank, cultivates prize flowers in the gardening club, and works on improving his drawing skills in the evening may have several fate lines, each originating from a different part of the palm. Likewise, the determined mother of four children who also climbs mountains, trained to climb Mt Everest, and, when her children had grown, published a poetic book about women in the mountains, may also have several fate lines. When we see multiple concurrent fate lines, we know that person puts consistent effort into diverse interests. Look to see which fate line starts first, and so had the most support in childhood, and which finishes last, toward the fingers, indicating that this has become the dominant effort of maturity.

WHERE IT BEGINS

To understand the nature of the life effort described by the fate line, look for where it begins and also at the branches that feed into the life line. Like tributaries flowing into a river, all branches that flow into the fate line contribute to the quality and nature of our efforts.

If the fate line originates from the life line or has a branch that feeds into the life line from the mount of the Sun, the family's abilities, skills, interests, and values contribute heavily to this person's life purpose. He might follow in his father's footsteps, inheriting a business, or he might use family skills in a different direction. If there are no other signs of original thinking, he may have accepted his family's values without question, and not made his own decisions.

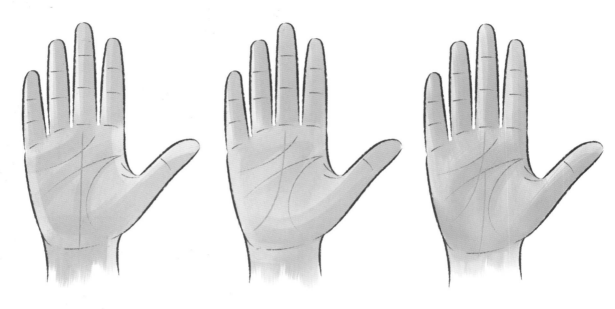

Fate line originates at the wrist and runs toward the mount of Saturn

Fate line originates in the mount of the Moon

Two fate lines

If the fate line originates at the wrist and runs in a straight line toward the mount of Saturn, this person has made up his own mind, leans toward self-reliance and resourcefulness, and takes practicalities into consideration.

A fate line that starts deep within the mount of the Moon indicates a person whose determination comes from his dreams or visions, his idealism or imagination.

It is common to see a branch from the mount of the Moon join a straight fate line midway, describing a person whose life starts off in a practical and family-approved way, but who has an inner idealistic or creative vision that merges with this practicality over time. For example, look at Barack Obama's fate line (see page 93), with two strong origins leading to one strong end.

Sometimes a person has two fate lines, one that extends upward from the wrist for a short way and then stops, and one that begins on the mount of the Moon and takes over the upward course. This is someone who is likely to be successful in visionary or creative work in the last part of his life. For example, a person working in a plastics factory who sculpts at the weekends may rise steadily in his job until the sculpting career becomes strong enough to end the factory work and take over as his main occupation.

RIGHT: Here, a deep, long, straight fate line starts on the mount of the Moon. This person found inspiration or direction early on from his own muse, his own psyche, and pursued it steadily. If he changes jobs, his inner direction stays constant. He pours energy into the world with his hands—note the wide, spatulate fingernails, as well as the obvious calluses and garden grime.

THE FATE LINE IN RELATION TO THE OTHER MAJOR LINES

It's easier on us if our fate, head, and heart lines match in depth and strength. This suggests a good work/life balance with physical strength to match our dreams. If the fate line is much deeper and stronger than the life line or heart line, this person may subsume his personal life into his professional life. If a dominant hand's fate line is stronger and the life and heart lines weaker than on the non-dominant hand, workaholic behavior may wear on health and happiness.

If all lines are stronger on the dominant rather than the non-dominant hand, career may keep this person alive and give him the energy to continue improving his situation.

To balance: Any extremes between the major lines and the fate line are indicative of the need to balance efforts made. A weak fate line means that person should concentrate on achieving healthy success in his life. A fate line that is stronger than the other major lines calls for effort to be shared evenly between work, home, and health.

MINOR LINES AND MARKS

Flesh out the picture

First we looked at the landscape of a hand and studied its proportions, strength, and contours. Then we sketched out the roadmap of major lines for the story of our lives. Now we fill in the picture through the sculpting and shading of subtle lines and markings.

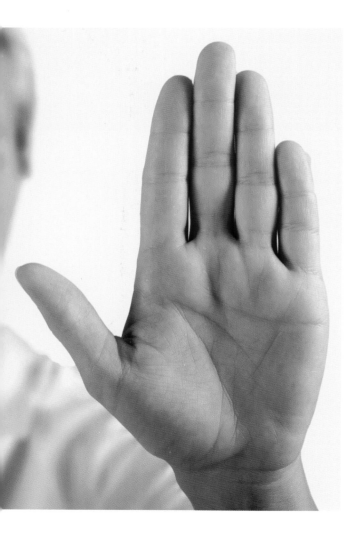

In general, lines that flow from the wrist toward the fingers are supportive lines that help us push our energy out to the world. Lines that come off the life line or head line and ascend toward the fingers usually denote moments of success or of extra support for that line and for its owner's efforts.

Lines that cross the palm (other than the major lines) have blocking energy. Sometimes they signify occasions when we had to accept a dead end and turn around. Sometimes they tell of important events that challenged us. Not all blocking lines are bad—overcoming them gives us the opportunity to grow from the experience.

LEFT: This kind and caring hand (a rounded oval palm with pointed fingertips and subtle overall lines) belongs to a sensitive soul. A Mercury line formed by a bundle of small lines underlines her intuition and ability to sense and express what is going on with the people around her, all characteristics that would help if she is in a healing profession. However, her health may be affected by her surroundings and stress levels; it would be good for her to develop healthy boundaries in relationships.

THE MERCURY LINE

How we diagnose and articulate our perceptions

This starts somewhere in the base of the palm and extends toward the mount of Mercury and the little finger. It may be deep and clear, or comprise many minor lines working together. Traditional astrology books often refer to it as a health, hepatic, or liver line, but the Mercury line is more about a certain form of energetic communication, a graphic example of our mind-body connection. It reflects how our nervous system is aware of our energetic surroundings and expresses how we experience that intuition. It is a conduit of energy flowing out through the most intimate, least public quadrant of the hand.

To have no Mercury line is considered a good sign. It implies a sturdy nervous system, and health that is not sensitive to surroundings, mood swings, or experiences. It may also imply a lack of that subtle physical intuition that improves our empathy with lover, client, or friend. It also suggests a potentially straightforward approach to communications (particularly when accompanied by a level head line), one that does not use metaphor, introspection, or evocative language.

A Mercury line composed of a wiry bundle of small lines signifies a sensitive nervous system that responds quickly, and a person who may think in gestalts or systems more than in linear format. People with this kind of Mercury line may have a versatile, responsive, eclectic communication style and use metaphor and symbols, but it may take them a little while to get to the point. These wiry little lines relate to

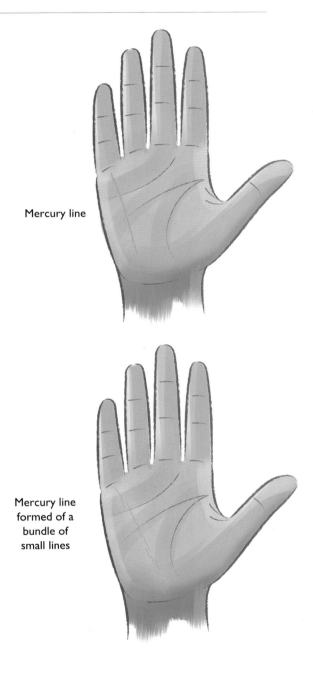

Mercury line

Mercury line formed of a bundle of small lines

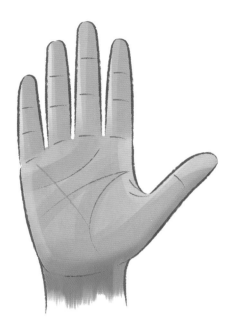

Mercury line originates
from the life line

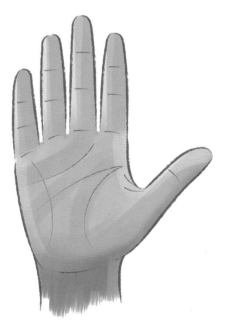

Mercury line originates from
the mount of the Moon

one another to form the Mercury line, and those who have this bundled version see relationships between symbols and concepts, cause and effect. Their health may be affected by their mood and by their response to those around them. They can get a headache from being with other people who have a headache, owing to their natural empathy, until they realize where it is coming from.

Their ability to digest both information and nutrients may respond to their moods. It's good for them to support their respiratory and digestive systems, gall, and liver. Intestinal problems can be something to keep an eye on if the middle, Saturn finger has a bend in the first knuckle that tilts the top two sections toward the little finger.

A deep, strong Mercury line tells of a clear communication style, deep focus, and the ability to think linearly. These people may be just as sensitive to their surroundings as those with a bundled Mercury line, but they are not thrown off by it. It is considered a sign of sturdy health, and they may give more energy than they receive.

WHERE IT BEGINS

If the Mercury line sprouts from the life line, inherited health problems may be a concern. Contrary to what some palmistry systems report, this meeting of the two lines does not correlate with a time of death. It does mean the owner would be well served if he learned to read the body's subtle signals and to listen to the delicate nuances of body health, the gut intuition that tells you when to relax, when to leave a toxic situation, and how to de-stress. If not, this person's health may become one of his psyche's main ways of communicating, and health issues can get louder and louder until the messages get across.

A Mercury line that sprouts from the mount of the Moon is a sign of strong intuition, and even more so if it creates a crescent around the mount. Again, this person may notice the intuition kinesthetically, that is feel it as a sensation in the body or in his health, but the information may come in more from intuitive awareness of the people around him than from his own nervous system.

To balance: Physicalized empathy can be balanced by taking an holistic approach to health, and learning to manage stress and anxiety. Becoming aware of the body's sensitive intuition is a first step to learning how not to take on the pain of others. A basic class on intuition can help to sort out the signals received and develop the ability to safeguard health.

If the Mercury line sprouts independently, it is indicative of an original, independent intelligence that synthesizes both logical and intuitive information and communicates with flexibility and fluency. This Mercury line provides less information about health than other Mercury lines, but does suggest that mind and body are deeply entwined. Mood affects health and health affects mood, and they must be treated together.

A double Mercury line acts as insulation for the nervous system and can strengthen health. In a nervous, thin, or pale hand, it supports health and adds robustness. In a sturdy, fleshy, or sensual hand, it can bring a desire to have the senses stimulated in order to break through the insulation and feel more intensely.

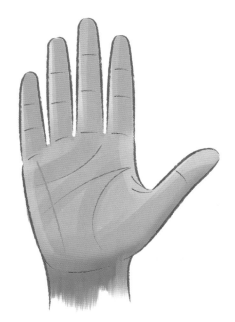

Mercury line starts independently

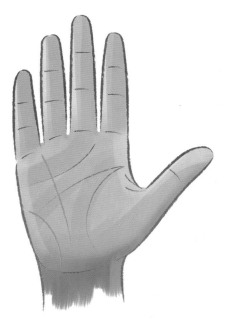

Double Mercury line

THE MERCURY CLUSTER

Look on the mount of Mercury, just under the little finger, for a series of little lines. They could appear to be part of the top of the Mercury line, or they could be standing free. They signify an ability to diagnose a problem and find a creative solution. While we most often see this cluster on a doctor's or healer's hand, we can also find it on a social critic's hand, an engineer's, a good therapist's, or on the hand of someone who knows how to be a good friend in a tough place. People who have a Mercury cluster can use their capacity in any field of real interest. They just understand what's wrong, and usually have a good idea about how to make it right.

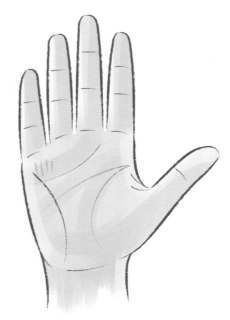

Mercury cluster

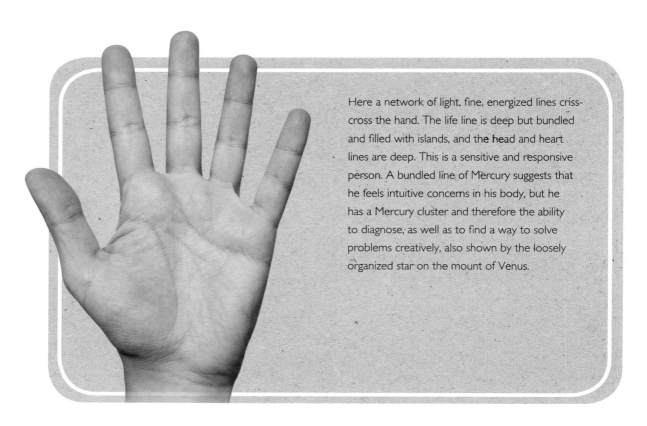

Here a network of light, fine, energized lines criss-cross the hand. The life line is deep but bundled and filled with islands, and the head and heart lines are deep. This is a sensitive and responsive person. A bundled line of Mercury suggests that he feels intuitive concerns in his body, but he has a Mercury cluster and therefore the ability to diagnose, as well as to find a way to solve problems creatively, also shown by the loosely organized star on the mount of Venus.

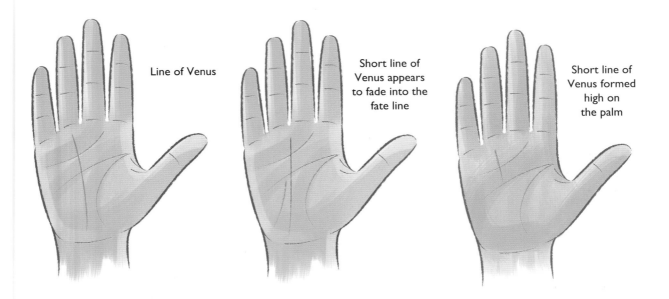

Line of Venus

Short line of Venus appears to fade into the fate line

Short line of Venus formed high on the palm

THE LINE OF VENUS

Heart and art

Traditionally known as the line of Apollo, the line of Venus is a conduit for successful talent. It acts as sister to the fate line and helps to channel energy from the wrist toward the mount and finger of creativity and personal charm. This is an extra line, and not everybody has it. Most of us have little threads that run in that direction, rather than a clear line. Read the quality of this line in relation to the quality of the hand's other lines. On a hand full of little lines, these threads are a sign of easy energy moving in that creative direction, but may not be highly significant by themselves. If we are looking at a hand with very few, simple, clear lines, even a short, definite Venus line speaks volumes about a particular time in that person's life when he found a clear conduit for his creative energy or personal magnetism, a time when he may have written a book or run for office.

A short Venus line from the lunar mound at the bottom of the palm that stops or appears to fade into the fate line may denote a person who was charming and creative as a child but who did not make the effort to keep the creative conduit open and has successfully settled into a pragmatic job. If a short Venus line forms high on the palm, traveling from the middle of the plane up toward the ring finger, it denotes a maturing talent that blooms later in life. This person may coalesce life knowledge into a creative form, such as writing, music, or an ability to manage people in a particularly inventive and personal way.

The Venus line brings charm, and with it, luck. It is often strong in people who have inherited money or family support and so have a sense of entitlement or confidence plus the generosity to share what they have. It's also strong in those charismatic people who just bring an

extra creative spark to all they do, and those
with an artistic talent and disposition who may,
compulsively, never do the same thing twice
but need to put their own personal stamp and
creative twist on all they do. A deep Venus line
with an extra long Venus finger is indicative of
someone who can often get away with using
flirtatious charm when simple hard work would
do. It can coincide with histrionic personalities
for whom emotions overwhelm logic and
melodrama replaces real feeling.

To balance: Those with a missing Venus line or
one that is faint and composed of disconnected
threads should consider taking some form
of creative craft or art class to help build up
confidence for imaginative expression. It should
be something they can enjoy approaching
as a beginner, whether decorating, writing,
improvised theater, pottery, dance, or guitar
lessons. Results are less important than taking
the opportunity for experimentation and
encouraging the creative process. Their growing
confidence will be reflected in the increasing ease
they feel in problem-solving and relating
to the world.

Those with an overdeveloped Venus line
should consider the hard-working people who
bring stability to our everyday lives, and nurture
levelheaded characteristics, such as physical
stamina, logic, and common sense, to create a
sound vessel for their creative spark. They should
try to develop solid personal routines so that their
creative spirit can be directed wholly into their
chosen art form and not into reinventing how to
wash dishes or make a bed every day.

MICK JAGGER

Mick Jagger has a long and well-developed
fate line, Venus line, and Mercury line. He has a
jagged Neptune line, and a faint girdle of Venus
(see opposite). Notice the strong beginnings of
his head, heart, and fate lines. He broke out of
the gates early and achieved enduring creative
success. He has a strong thumb and a well-
developed mount of the Sun, indicating that he
has strong physical endurance and willpower to
back that creativity. He has a deep but relatively
short heart line, and no clearly visible lines of
affection (see page 107). It looks as though he
has poured his emotional energy into his career
and formed lasting bonds with his bandmates,
but may not have bonded quite as easily in
romance. He lives his work, and it has added
strength and length to his life.

THE GIRDLE OF VENUS
Emotional excitability

Look for a line or series of lines bundled together to form a crescent underlying and isolating the Saturn and Venus fingers. Most people don't have one. This secondary heart line indicates an emotionally responsive personality, with a certain soul hunger that needs a lot of stimulation to let its owner know he's alive. This line cuts off or buffers the flow to the Venus and Saturn fingers, so it can be hard for people who do have a girdle of Venus to feel deeply connected, and they often seek out unusual or heightened experiences to break through this sense of isolation. While the line traditionally has a bad reputation as being a sign of debauchery, that's a painful misconception. These people love restlessly and passionately, and may run through relationships seeking intensity, but they're really searching for an experience or substantial love that will reach into their isolation and help them feel connected.

This experimental restlessness can lead to an extraordinary life. These people have wrestled with their own extra emotional charge and problematic feelings, and so often have a high emotional intelligence and know what's going on with others. Their often turbulent emotional lives may not make sense from the outside. They may leave jobs or relocate for the sake of love, or walk away from old friends during a break-up. Without active feedback, they can have trouble trusting in their own self-worth, and others can find them needy as a result. If life does not give them the charge they need, they can become moody, depressed, and, particularly with a drooping

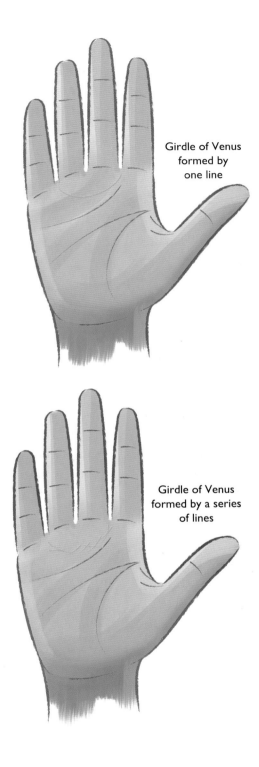

Girdle of Venus formed by one line

Girdle of Venus formed by a series of lines

LEFT: This man touching
his baby's hand is opening
his heart to a new form
of love, one that may
help calm the emotional
restlessness indicated
by the girdle of Venus
visible in his hand. Intense
experiences always affect
his heart; his girdle of
Venus has breaks in it,
which are openings to
let him connect.

head line, even suicidal. They don't want to die; they just want life to be seriously different. They may find it tricky to settle into a long-term relationship, but when they do, it can be deeply healing and they can form a profound attachment.

This line is also found in highly creative people who, healthfully, pour their passion into their music or art form, as well as in altruists who feel most alive when they respond to emergencies. For artists, performance artists, musicians, and public speakers, a girdle of Venus adds charisma as they work to reach across the divide, even if it contributes to that well-known artistic temperament.

It takes common sense to balance the emotional voltage, so this line is safer with a strong head line and is more dangerous with a wobbly head line. If it is less defined on the dominant hand, the owner is healing, growing out

of his emotional volatility. If it is clearer cut and contiguous on the dominant hand, then he may be pursuing emotional stimulation to his detriment, and can feel addicted to romance or sex as a replacement for real love.

To balance: People who need to balance these emotional extremes should look for healthy creative expression, and notice the difference between restlessly searching for stimulation and true curiosity. They should try to be more open to receiving what is here rather than always looking for something just beyond the horizon, and learn to slow down and seek that deeper connection to spirit. Relationships may then begin to settle down, become more nourishing, and feed that deep soul hunger.

LINES OF AFFECTION
Capacity to bond

Lines of affection wrap around from the private side of the hand under the little finger at the edge of the mount of Mercury. These lines were traditionally called the marriage lines, and after the life line are the second place many people look. They correlate with our capacity to bond and care deeply, but not necessarily with our marriages. They are indicative of the ability to connect with mental and emotional honesty and intimacy, at heart and soul level, regardless of gender or romance, and certainly regardless of legal marriage, and so are always a good sign for one's love life. They are to do with the skills needed to form a rich and healthy partnership bond, and so can help mitigate the restlessness of a girdle of Venus, or the reserve of a short heart line.

However, it is quite possible for someone to be happily married and care for his children, family, or church, and not have any lines of affection. Occasionally, you may see little lines that run parallel with the lines of affection and match the number of children in that relationship, but not always. If a person never marries, but has long-standing, deep, and abiding romances, or a few best friends with whom he walks through life, we also see several lines of affection.

One long, deep line means that, although this is someone who may have other relationships before or after marriage, his predisposition is to bond once and be married for life. If a person has a series of lines of affection, he has the capacity to love more than one person. Whether he is a serial monogamist and loves one person at a time,

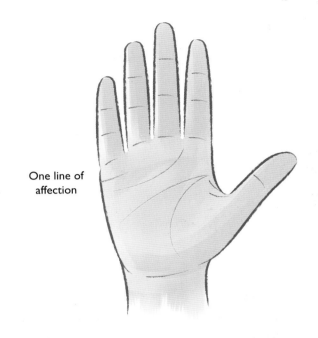

One line of affection

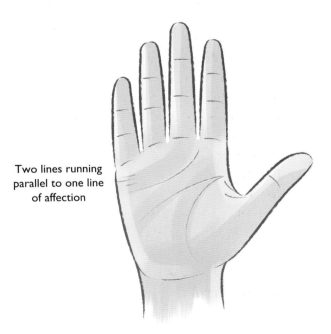

Two lines running parallel to one line of affection

or a polyamorist and able to love more than one person at the same time, his heart has complex karmic relationships. The closer to the heart line that the affection lines begin, the earlier the relationships form. The higher up toward the Mercury finger the affection lines form, the later in life the owner may bond.

These patterns hold true regardless of gender or sexual preference—to love is to love in palmistry. If people experience trauma or intolerance in response to being gay or not conforming to gender as a child, that may show up as crossing event lines, islands, or a short, reserved heart line. But those signs are a response to the intolerance they may have been subjected to, and are not linked with the heart. There are no clear indicators to do with people loving their own gender, or feeling they are not truly the gender they were assigned at birth.

Some people have no lines of affection but a very long and strong heart line, which shows similar capacity to bond. This may describe a good marriage but one in which partners live parallel lives to an extent, and don't necessarily need to communicate everything to their mate. If a person has no affection lines, no girdle of Venus, a small mount of the Sun, and a short heart line, don't wait for him to propose. Human connection may or may not happen, but it is not the point of this life for him.

ABOVE: This is the hand of someone who is articulate, indicated by the long little finger, and an independent thinker—a clean, focused head line originates separately from the life line. She has a warm heart with an altruistic, idealistic streak. It gives her emotional satisfaction to help humankind. This is indicated by the long Venus finger with a clear heart line that runs into the Jupiter finger. She also has the capacity to form long-term, deep, personal relationships, as shown by a strong line of affection on the mount of Mercury. However, she may find a partner later in life—that affection line is closer to the finger of Mercury than to her heart line.

THE NEPTUNE LINE
Buffering our sensitivities

Traditionally called a poison line, this is a sharp line or contiguous collection of finer lines that run around from the private side of the hand and cut off the bottom of the mount of the Moon, the root of intuitions and dreams that we call the mount of Neptune. We can think of the mount of Neptune as our well, a source of inspiration, like the Pythian well at the Oracle of Delphi. It is helpful to have the Venus or Mercury line springing from Neptune, or a network of fine lines running up from Neptune toward the fingers, because these act as conduits from the well, bringing inspiration and intuition to our practical lives.

Sometimes, though, especially with a full mount of the Moon and Neptune, this part of the psyche can become so active that it's uncomfortable, and the feeling of being overloaded may lead to a need for insulation. A Neptune line can buffer access to that tender corner, but often at a cost. People in this situation may experience vivid dreams, but have trouble remembering them. Like someone with a strong Mercury line, they may intuit what's going on around them, but instead of becoming conscious of it, feel it in their bodies. This can produce subtle health issues related to leaky boundaries, such as allergies and auto-immune problems as a result of becoming too permeable to certain pollens, proteins, or yeasts. It can also trigger a desire to insulate sensitivities with alcohol, drugs, or other escapist habits.

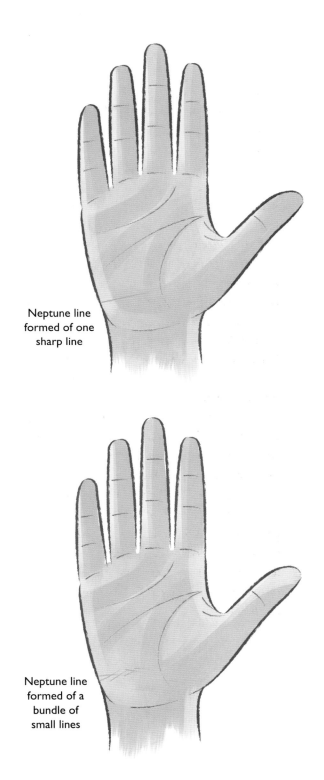

Neptune line formed of one sharp line

Neptune line formed of a bundle of small lines

It can be helpful to have a Neptune line to protect a tender and permeable psyche, but we can be more comfortable if we learn to hold strong health boundaries consciously.

To balance: Minimizing exposure to food or environmental sensitivities is the first thing to suggest; then strengthening the body's immune and digestive systems. The psyche can be helped to find another way to manage sensitivity and intuition, by the person taking a class on intuitive development that focuses on psychic defenses, for example. Therapy helps to deal with escapist habits. Someone with this problem should concentrate on finding healthy ways to de-stress, understanding clean boundaries, and cultivating a sense of personal responsibility.

ABOVE: This hand has a faint square (see opposite) under the Jupiter finger—this person is a natural philosopher and teacher. Note the success lines coming off his life line in the middle of his life, and a fate line that begins about a third of the way up from the bottom, both of which suggest that his understanding and ability to teach developed through his life experience and found form in his maturity. He also has a faint Neptune line that blocks the lower part of his lunar mount, suggesting that once upon a time he had trouble trusting his intuition, experienced allergies, or had been gently fond of forms of escapism. These potential escapist habits have not yet badly affected his life—the life line, head line, and heart line stay strong. A comparison of his dominant and non-dominant hands would show if these habits are getting worse or improving.

MARKS THAT ENRICH OUR LANDSCAPE

Squares, stars, triangles, crosses, and islands

After you've examined the rolling hills of the hand's landscape and mapped the major lines, notice any unusual markings, particularly those that are freestanding and not formed by the crossing of other lines. Look on the main lines for markings that stand out. Again, markings on a very busy hand may read not as individual events or experiences, but as an example of a fertile and responsive approach to the world. Markings on a clear hand with few lines are significant, relating to a specific event or characteristic. They all add texture and fill in the unique picture presented by the hand.

Remember that lines that flow out toward the fingers are helpful, supportive lines that conduct energy out to the world. Lines that come off the life line or head line and ascend toward the fingers usually signify moments of success or times of extra support for that line and for the person's efforts.

Crossing lines have a blocking energy. They tell of challenging events that had an overall positive effect on the person's life because they enabled him to grow, but are not what he would have asked for.

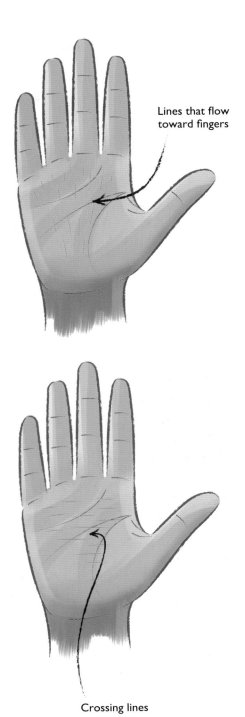

Lines that flow toward fingers

Crossing lines

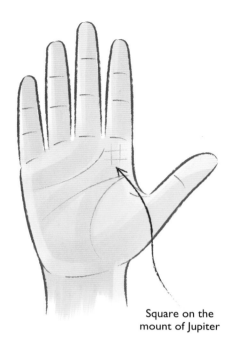

Square on the
mount of Jupiter

SQUARES

These are formed by intersecting but independent lines and often look like scaffolding or bracing. They are usually located on a specific mount and act as protection and strength-stabilizers.

• Mount of Jupiter: the ability to teach, to present material in an organized and sound way, and confidence in public speaking.

• Mount of Saturn: generalized protection of life and an ability to think rationally in a crisis.

• Mount of Venus: artistic competence and recognition.

• Mount of Mercury: inherent sanity and protection from the effects of other people's dishonesty.

• The only place a square has a questionable meaning is on the lower mount of Mars, where it can mean both general control of the temper, and a cyst of old angry memories that can bring extra intensity or violence to an argument if that cyst is triggered. Once the person is conscious of his triggers, the effects of that square begin to soften and heal.

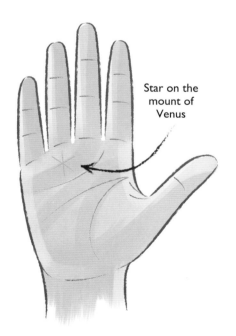

Star on the
mount of
Venus

STARS

Stars formed by three or more lines have a mixed reputation. The confusion of lines amounts to a potential-filled concentration of energy. A freestanding star on a particular mount can become a source of energy and success if the person consciously finds a way to express it, or a source of frustrated disappointment and poor judgment if he doesn't.

• Mount of Jupiter: a desire to be famous; may have complex relationships with the public and with well-connected people.

• Mount of Mars: extra flammability of temper and spark of charisma.

• Mount of Saturn: angst about life-purpose, possibly in response to a challenging major event, and a tendency to a melancholic if philosophic disposition.

• Mount of Venus: the ability to turn life's complexities into artistic inspiration, and the possibility of becoming well known, or notorious, for the resulting work.

• Mount of Mercury: a possibly complex and problematic sense of truth, and the ability articulately to influence others, for better or worse.

• A major line: suggestion of crisis but with opportunity. If a star comes at the end of a major line, the crisis could have real danger.

To balance: A star always brings complications, and the job of the person who has one can be to keep his priorities straight and simplify the situation by exercising common sense and compassion. The soul's priorities act as a lighthouse and a guide through choppy waters so that the most can be made of unusual and challenging circumstances.

TRIANGLES

As stable as squares, triangles are more flowing in effect. They signify a talent to be encouraged, a way of juggling doubts and gifts to produce good work. This is a resource, a place of ease, but it's up to the person to use that talent and tap the resource.

• Mount of Jupiter: diplomacy.

• Mount of Mars: physical energy and a talent for strategy and winning an argument.

• Mount of the Moon or Neptune: intuitive dreams and a love of the sea or a need to be near water.

• Mount of Mercury: a touch of the Blarney Stone, poetic verbal fluency that can help mitigate other signs.

• Mount of Venus: practical creative ingenuity.

• Mount of Saturn: an aptitude for the sciences or the occult, the ability to see patterns in the world in a chosen field of interest.

• On a major line, if free-form rather than formed by a series of draining and success lines, triangles suggest an opportunity to engage talent successfully.

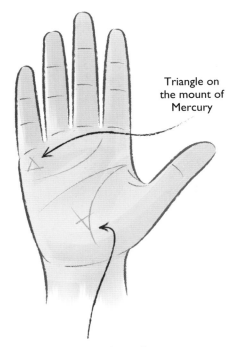

Triangle on the mount of Mercury

Triangle on the life line

CROSSES

These show burdens to be borne. Look for free-floating crosses, not the random crossing of other major lines. A cross blocks the flow. On a major line, a cross describes a difficult event that interrupted the person's life story. On a mount, a cross tells of a block in expression, self-defeating habits that may stem from some early difficult event. Look to see if these crosses are connected to event lines traversing the life line. This describes a time when the owner lost confidence through confrontation or test, internalized the pattern, and so tends not to believe in himself, undermining his own efforts.

- Mount of Mercury: difficulty in speaking the truth.
- Mount of Mars: irritable aggression in response to difficulties.
- Mount of the Moon or Neptune: a clear cross shows a propensity to get lost in inner worlds, or a will to hold on to deep, early hurt, which at some point will start to distort perception.
- Mount of Venus: lack of creative confidence and writer's block.
- Mount of Saturn: a wrestling mind that can argue itself into an ulcer.
- Crosses networking between the head and heart lines on the great quadrangle are different. They map an interconnection between head and heart and between right and left sides of the brain, and are considered signs of intuition or interest in the occult or paranormal phenomena. The owner sees things differently from other people and may feel like the odd person out until he comes to enjoy his unique perspective.

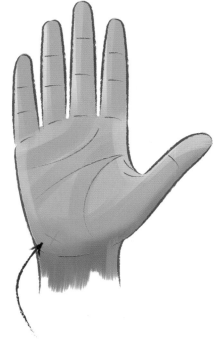

Cross on the mount of the Moon

To balance: Any difficult crosses can be counteracted by noticing how self-defeating patterns are created in the mind, and finding ways of expressing energies clearly.

ISLANDS

These are usually found on lines, but sometimes they appear as a circle or oval formed by minor lines around an empty space. All islands tell of a time or place of isolation or feeling cut off. They can also imply protection, a choice to insulate or isolate because circumstances were dangerous or uncomfortable. A person with a pronounced island on the earlier part of a major line may have spent time in childhood in a deep inner world to avoid a parent's alcoholic behavior or other dangerous chaos. If there is an island on the heart line but not on the head or life line, this person may have chosen to go into his mind to avoid an emotionally uncomfortable situation, and managed just fine. If the island is on the head line but not the heart or life line, he may have felt unable to communicate with people nearby, but expressed himself through acts of compassion and creativity, which helped him to break out of that sense of isolation.

To balance: A person whose hand has an island would benefit from creating a healthy and safe connection with the world, and it may help to talk about it. You could encourage this by speaking compassionately about the possible isolation if the island appears in the past. If it appears in the future, mention finding ways to feel protected without separation. Talk about the difference between the gift of solitude and the wall of isolation, and discuss potential ways to stay safely connected and engaged.

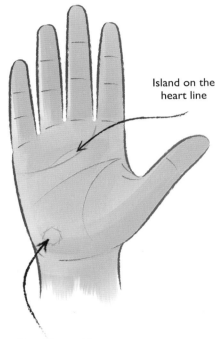

Island on the heart line

Island formed by minor lines

PART III

PUTTING IT ALL TOGETHER

OBSERVING HANDS

When you start studying hands, it's important to stay humble and not to make radical assumptions about your sitters. If you are starting with family and friends, you will know quite a lot about them already, of course, but otherwise it's fine to form an hypothesis about what the people whose hands you are observing may be like and what might be the best way to interact with them. If you have the chance to get to know the owners of these hands, watch them over time, and let them teach you about palmistry as you correlate how they are with what you see.

By now I hope you have picked up the habit of glancing at all the hands you meet. If you're a counselor, artist, healer, or police officer, or work in human resources, you probably have more time and permission to look at people's hands than

most of us, but anyone can develop the habit. Now that you know where to look, notice the landscape of the hand through simple handshakes or as a person hands you your mail or purchase. Observe fingernails, proportions of the hand, its skin texture and thumb.

If you know the person well enough to hold his hand, check its flexibility and look at the lines. We find so many combinations of lines on the human hand that it can be confusing for a budding palmist. The diagram on page 118 may provide a helpful checklist, or, even better, trace the outline of the hand itself.

Take notes about the texture of each person's hand, its flexibility and shape and the shape of the fingernails, and whether the mounts are prominent or underdeveloped. Note whether the hand leads straight from the arm, and whether the palm and fingers tilt toward the public or private side of the hand. Stop there for a moment to think about what this information tells you. Remember that this landscape of the hand tells you much about how to deal with this person right away, as well as laying the foundation to interpret all the lines and finer markings. Keep notes on the non-dominant as well as the dominant hand. Comparisons between the two are often helpful.

Before you go any farther, sketch the pattern of the life, head, and heart lines, and think about each one in relation to the shape and form of the hand. This is the skeleton upon which to build your understanding of all the other markings and lines. Think about the nature of the person's life force as seen in his life line, and about the nature of his thinking, focus, and attitude as expressed by his head line. Explore the nature of his emotions as seen in the heart line.

Then note the quality, or absence, of a fate line, Venus line, Mercury line, Neptune line, and girdle of Venus, and think about those in relation to the basic framework. Finally, look for unusual markings, squares, stars, event lines, or any of the others you've read about in the previous pages. If the hand is clean and clear with few but deep lines, every little marking is significant. If the hand is full of wiry little lines, interpret any markings you find in relation to this pattern, and question if it is a true marking or just the versatility and electricity of personality coming through.

If you can, ask your subject about the quality of his relationship with his family and work, and about major events in his life, and see if you can find markings on his hand that correlate.

Once you can mark the time of a major success, disappointment, or danger on the life line, you get a sense of timing on that hand. Remember that each hand shows timing in a unique and subjective way; for some people, the events of their childhood could stretch way into the middle of the hand, and their middle years and older age are compacted. For others, the markings of childhood go by in a flash and the events of young adulthood are marked close to the beginning of the life line. We appear to stretch out our subjective sense of time depending upon what part of our life contributed most to our personal evolution or engaged us the most, and to compact the markings when life proceeds as usual.

COLLECTING HANDS

Consider starting your own collection of hand images of people you know. Compare each person's hand with the original image every few years, or a few months after major life events, and watch for changes in the lines and shape of the hand over time. The changes may be subtle, but our minds shrink and grow, the fine lines increase or decrease depending upon how we live our life. The bones of our hands don't change in length or width, but they do shift in relation to one another, and whether they lean in or lean out, and that can change how long the fingers appear in proportion to one another.

The most complete and durable form of hand imagery is to take an impression of the hand in clay, as celebrities do along walkways and so many children do in their early school years to bring home to their parents. But these are messy, and tricky to store.

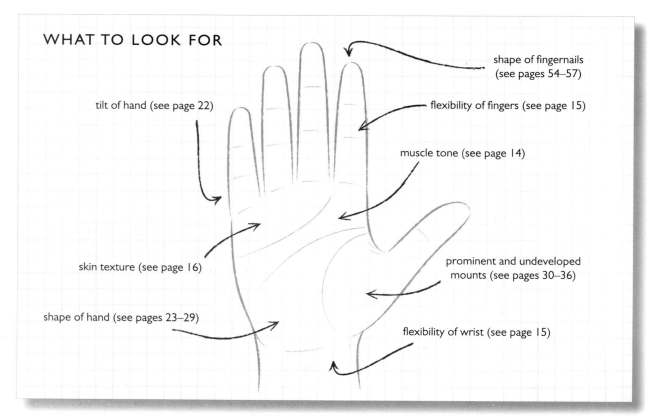

WHAT TO LOOK FOR

shape of fingernails (see pages 54–57)

tilt of hand (see page 22)

flexibility of fingers (see page 15)

muscle tone (see page 14)

skin texture (see page 16)

prominent and undeveloped mounts (see pages 30–36)

shape of hand (see pages 23–29)

flexibility of wrist (see page 15)

The clearest impression, as the police have found, is to take an ink print of the hand. Washable, baby-safe ink for handprints can be found online. It's used to record babies' feet and handprints for sentimental and safety reasons, but works very well for the budding palmist.

I have found the easiest way to print hands is to use water-soluble woodblock ink and an ink roller. This is the easiest to wash off, too. Run the roller back and forth through a small daub of woodblock ink until you get a thin, even coat on the roller. Ink your subject's hand thoroughly, taking care to cover the middle of the palm and the fingertips. Place the hand on a piece of paper, press down on the middle so that the center lines print, and roll the fingertips to get clear fingerprints. Then trace the hand, and draw the

shape of the fingernails above each finger. Hold the paper down while your subject picks up his hand to prevent smudging. Write his name and the date on the paper so that you can compare with future handprints and note changes. Then do the other hand. Take notes about your sitter's personality and life story, and see how the notes compare with what you see in his hands.

It is most convenient to take photos of hands and store them on the computer. It can be hard to see the fine lines clearly unless you take high-resolution pictures and use the computer to magnify the lines. For the best clarity, take photos of both sides of the hand. Position a bright light at an oblique angle to the hand—a little bit of shadow will help you to see the lines more clearly.

CASE HISTORIES

*Here are two case histories. See where I got my information, make your
own observations, then read the feedback from the hand's owner.*

THE THOUGHTFUL WOMAN

In this study, we are analyzing the palm-side only
of the dominant hand of Sarah (photo on page
120). For even greater insight, this reading would
be combined with readings of the back of the
hand and of her non-dominant left hand.

Sarah's hand is busy, full of wiry little lines.
Remember to interpret any markings you find
in relation to this pattern and ask whether it is
significant, or is just the versatility and electricity
of her multi-tasking personality being expressed.

THE LANDSCAPE OF THE HAND

This is the hand of someone who feels events
deeply and thinks them through—notice the
fine-grained skin and network of lines, long, thin
fingers, reddish fingertips with sensitive points on
the pads, and a somewhat concave palm—but has
common sense underlying her sensitivity, seen in
her rectangular palm.

She expresses herself diplomatically and
kindly, and pays great attention to detail: she has
rounded fingertips on long fingers, unusually long
Venus and Mercury fingers, and an active Venus
line. A healthy mount of the Sun suggests she
has good reserves of energy, but it is expressed
through her mind more than her physicality—her
palm is narrower at the base, wider at the top.

Her fingers soak up both practical and
intuitive information, but she then evaluates this
information with reasonably skeptical logic—her

fingers are smooth through the first knuckle, then
knot at the second. She has healthy willpower, but
is carefully diplomatic about imposing that will on
others: her thumb has a strong, angular knuckle
and a long bottom section. The top thumb section
is of average length but somewhat pointed, while
the lower mount of Mars is deep but flat—she
doesn't anger quickly, but tends to remember
hurts from others, as well as her own mistakes.
You cannot push her where she doesn't want
to go; she'll quietly hold her ground, but will
respect your autonomy.

Jupiter—long, relatively straight, with sections
of roughly equal length, gently curving inward:
her relationship with the public is open and
comfortable, but she has the introvert's need
for quiet time. Note the strong teacher's square
on the mount of Jupiter: she can teach what she
knows.

Saturn—sensitive, somewhat pointed fingertip
and whorl fingerprint: she thinks for herself
and mulls over her experience to understand
the situation. She has a relatively pragmatic
philosophy and her professional life is important
to her. When she feels stress, she may need
to eat carefully: the finger tilts in at the first
knuckle, the sections are roughly the same but the
midsection is the largest, and there is a crossed
line on the mount of Saturn.

Venus—unusually long with a teardrop
fingerprint: while she can be a natural leader

THE ROADMAP OF THE HAND

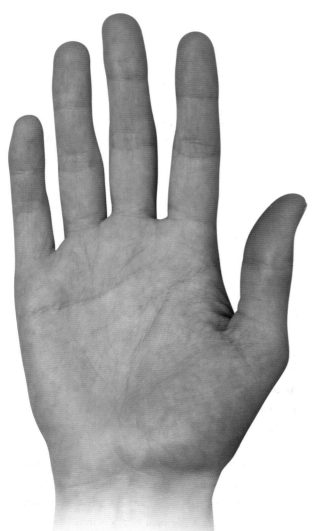

She's always been a sensitive person; when she was young, her sense of self was affected by familial opinion (seen in the chained early life line with drooping lines underneath), but early success in school or community helped her to define herself—note the early success lines coming off the life line towards Jupiter.

Her early fate line is composed of a series of loosely correlated fine lines, starting in the center, meaning she started off closer to her family's concerns, while her later fate is a loosely woven array of many relatively deep lines that originate in the lunar mount and head toward the Saturn finger—it took her a while to find her own path. Her nervous system and health were affected by sensitivities earlier on in life, and she may have blocked her intuition so as not to pick up quite so much—there are many sensitive lines, and a Neptune line crosses her lower lunar mount. However, her vitality improves as her life goes on: the life, head, heart, Venus, and fate lines all strengthen as they go along, suggesting that the second half of her life looks healthier, stronger, more self-determined, and more focused than the first.

Her thinking is both pragmatic and inspired, and she has an interest in recent history: her straight head line has a branch that dips toward a historian's bump on the upper lunar mount. There is an island on the head line—some events left her feeling isolated in her late adolescence to early adulthood—but she had layers of support around her (seen in faint, long guardian lines supporting the life line); she may have been professionally successful through this time, but was disinclined to trust for a while—success

among friends and colleagues, her close inner circle probably sees more of her warmth and eccentricity. She has a complex creative approach that develops over time, and can be known for what she produces: there is a star on her mount of Venus, and a bundled Venus line that strengthens higher in the palm.

Mercury—straight and long: she's honest, and needs absolute honesty from others; she also notices sounds, poetry, rhythms, and the quality of music. With diagnostician's lines, she quickly recognizes any problem and wants to fix it.

lines come up from the life line, through minor overlapping breaks, which are connected to the island on the head line via event lines.

She has a strong heart line with a branch between Jupiter and Saturn, as well as lines of affection: she has always had an altruistic side, a love for people in general though perhaps not persons in particular, and this kept her heart warm even when she was wary; she is quite capable of forming deep connections. Her heart line has branches that droop in early to mid-adolescence, a branch that reaches toward the mount of Jupiter, and a branch (with breaks) that reaches between Jupiter and Saturn, which all suggest that she is friendly if reserved when she first connects, but appreciates if the other extends themself to take the relationship to a deeper level. If she feels her trust or privacy is disrespected, she will retreat to polite reserve. If her trust is respected, she will never let you down.

ABOUT THE OWNER OF THE HAND

"I had never met Heather, yet identified with much of the description above: characteristics such as being comfortable with people but needing alone time afterwards, quietly holding my ground, introspection, and revealing my eccentricities only to my inner circle all rang very true for me. As a copy-editor and a musician, attention to detail and appreciation of sound and rhythm were spot on. My mother suffered from ill health in her teenage years and passed away just before I turned 17, arguably an isolating time for me, despite having familial support, but I have worked to heal many of those wounds since. I am in a happy and stable long-term relationship."

THE PRACTICAL CREATIVE

Here we look at both hands of Jamie (photo on page 123), offering a chance to see how her character has changed. Jamie's hands have few but deep, clear lines—the hands of someone who prefers to concentrate on one thing at a time; where almost every marking is significant.

THE LANDSCAPE OF THE HAND

This person cares deeply about people, and is generous with her heart and energy: the palms are square in the base, wide in the middle and curved at the top, creating a rounded square echoed in the fingernails. Strong musculature and calluses suggest manual efforts. A palm as wide as it is tall signifies action-orientation, but the proportion above the head and heart lines indicates an active mind. With well-developed lower finger sections, yet space to see between them, her approach is earthy, but not materially indulgent or attached.

A large mount of the Sun and a deep, long, arched life line suggest that she has great physical reserves and stamina. Earlier in life, she may have felt disempowered, but has come to have personal soul strength: the mount of Pluto is dented on the passive right hand, but stronger on the active left hand, along with a strong base of the active palm.

Although sensitive with a deep inner world —fine-grained skin, hairless hands, and a well-developed lunar mount with lines rising from it —she has unusually good common sense and an independent, if sensitively expressed, willpower: low-set thumbs with whorl fingerprints and strong lower sections but quite long, pointed upper sections. She has a slightly puffy but not deep Mars mount: a quick, if moderate, temper that doesn't hold on to resentments.

Jupiter—strong and straight, pointed fingertip and a short, square fingernail, plus a strong teacher's square on the left-hand Jupiter mount: she intuitively knows how to reach out to the public and is comfortable speaking and teaching publicly, although this skill was acquired rather than innate (there is no square on the passive right hand). Her way of connecting with the world was once more conventional and less secure, but she now expresses herself with natural simplicity: both Jupiter fingers are slightly short, and the passive Jupiter has a loop fingerprint, while on the active hand it has a tented-arch fingerprint. This is echoed by many lines flowing out toward the fingers, which can add charisma, but occasionally cause trouble with too direct speech.
Saturn—square fingernail, rounded fingertips with a loop print, and a bend at the first knuckle: she has a traditional philosophy, more spiritual than material, and tends to hold tension in the gut.
Venus—fairly long and strong, with a deeper rectangle fingernail: she takes a warm, idiosyncratic approach to social relationships. Note that both hands hold the little finger and forefinger gently apart but keep Saturn and Venus close together—she thinks and acts independently, but does not feel there are enough material resources to carry out all her ideas.
Mercury—unusually long upper section, rounded oblong fingernail, loop fingerprint: communication is particularly important to her in personal relationships, and her mind never stops working.

THE ROADMAP OF THE HAND

She was born a practical creative, but has really developed that inspired creativity over time—a Venus line is much stronger on the dominant left hand. A chained early life line indicates early childhood tangles and moments of isolation; then early success lines mix with crossing event lines, and minor breaks and islands appear on the life line until her early twenties, pointing to a mix of positive and challenging events in mid-childhood and a potential health crisis at the beginning of adolescence. Later, strong success lines reach up off the life line toward Jupiter: as her identity separated from family, there was more room for success. Around the same time, and again in the mid-thirties and early forties, events involving emotional identity or close relationships are difficult, but do not interrupt the mental equilibrium; this is indicated by event lines that cross from the mount of Mars over the life line and head line, hit a minor break in the heart line, and go toward Mercury.

Her head line is level, deep, and clear on the passive hand, but on the dominant hand, the head line has a three-forked ending (one level and two that arch deeper into the lunar and Neptune mounts): she has an uncluttered, focused mind and started out as a pretty levelheaded person, but her interests diversified over time, and more spiritual or emotional areas had an effect.

She has a strong heart line that arches up between Jupiter and Saturn, plus a long line of affection: she is able to connect easily and build a strong family life. Her career has always been a balancing act between intellect, creativity, and professionalism; on the passive hand, the fate line starts off strong from the life line, with branches toward Mercury, Venus, and Saturn. With diagnostician's and Mercury lines, she easily sees and solves problems. Her fate line is stronger

on the passive hand than on the active: she has potential yet to fulfill. She will be successful and adventurous in her work late into life: on the active hand, the fate, Venus, and Mercury lines get stronger, and the life line has a series of gentle success lines rising from it well into her sixties.

ABOUT THE OWNER OF THE HAND

"I felt the reading completely resonated with me. I grew up on a farm and still work with my hands in my spare time. When young, I developed a fascination with science and how things work, and was ambitious—so even though no one in my family had finished high school, I gained a scientific PhD and a postdoc at Harvard.

My early childhood was precarious; my birth parents were unable to care for me so I was adopted when I was four by my aunt and uncle and began working on their farm, going from danger to a loving, supportive environment. When I was 11, my appendix ruptured and nearly killed me.

I spent a lot of time learning to value myself. I used to be drawn to relationships with people who made me feel needed, but these were unhealthy, leading to difficult separations in my early twenties and mid-thirties. Throughout this period I worked in a laboratory, using hands and mind together, and enjoyed professional success as a professor. I had a long-standing urge to come to know my feminine side, and in my mid-forties I transitioned from male to female. I began to explore my Native American heritage and spirituality, and as a result became less interested in laboratory work and more concerned with how to broaden the concept of science and help students learn. I now work to transform multicultural science education so that students can bring their culture, spirit, minds and hearts into the classroom. I am happily married."

HAND MASSAGE

Palmistry-inspired hand massage is a way to integrate and internalize what you've learned, and use it to tune into your healthiest self.

According to Chinese medicine, a series of energy conduits run throughout the body, engaging all our organs, and have points on the hands and feet. Without diving into that complex medical system (although it is a worthy study; see Resources, page 128), we can use a simple self-massage process to understand our emotional tender places and balance and soothe our system. Massage one hand and then the other as firmly as is comfortable, and notice which fingers and parts are sensitive.

As you massage the ball of the thumb/mount of the Sun, imagine releasing tension and vitalizing your root energy and reserve of life force. As you massage the lunar mount, visualize massaging your deepest inner psyche and easing your dream world. As you work the palm of the hand/plain of Mars, visualize relaxing your daily relationships, soothing your workaday world, softening the workings of your inner organs, and easing the effect of your daily interactions. Now work on the mount of Pluto, that dent in the middle of the bottom of your palm, where the life line heads and the fate line starts, and as you massage this point, imagine relaxing your lower back and pelvis, renewing your sense of support, connecting yourself to your source.

The thumb is the symbol and gauge of our will, our control, common sense, and stubbornness. Massage your thumb and relax the tension and worry of being in control. Notice how sensitive, sore, or hungry for touch this thumb might be. As you work on, or gently hold, your thumb, imagine your stress melting, and contemplate the notion that we co-create our world with spirit: the reins of our life are in our hands, but the course is not up to us alone. Imagine being infused with a renewed sense of empowerment and co-creation.

We know the forefinger, the Jupiter finger, is our gauge of how we reach out to the world and digest our experience. As you massage or gently

RIGHT: This shows someone massaging the mount of the Moon and Neptune.

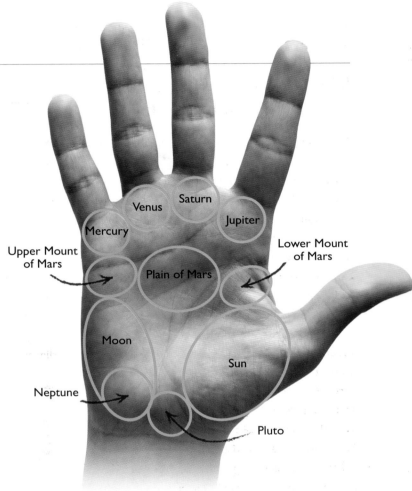

RIGHT: A reminder of the mounts, which are the main areas for massage.

hold the mount of Jupiter and your forefinger, imagine you're relaxing any fear of engaging with the world, supporting your digestion and clearing your mind. Feel your gut relaxing, and your confidence, calm, and self-acceptance returning.

The Saturn or middle finger is the gauge of our ability to hold center, to balance our inner and outer worlds and hold our personal authority. Massage your mount of Saturn and finger and imagine your anger and frustration leaving, along with any exhaustion from doing the work you came here to do. Imagine your work and private life coming into healthy balance, your liver and gallbladder feeling supported, and your calm, stamina, and good temperament returning.

The ring or Venus finger holds our creative energy and capacity for loving relationships, and carries a line to our emotional core. As you massage the mount and finger of Venus, imagine massaging away your sadness, soothing your relationships, easing your breathing and your heart, improving your attitude, and opening a conduit for your creativity to pour into the world.

The little finger, Mercury, is the symbol and gauge of our relationship to sound and music, our most intimate connections, and our connection to our own truth. As you hold or massage the mount and finger of Mercury, visualize releasing any scar tissue of old emotional defenses, call in comfortable and smooth intimate relationships, and imagine strengthening your capacity to speak your truth.

Finish by gently shaking the hands out, rubbing them together, and then feeling your thoughts, emotions, and good will flowing through your hands, out to the world. In return, feel the strength and healing of the natural world flowing back into you through the fingers and palms, and into your core.

INDEX

RESOURCES

Read further, using the list given here, and test out the theories for yourself.

BEGINNER TO INTERMEDIATE

The Book of the Hand: An Illustrated History of Palmistry by Fred Gettings (1968)

Hands: A Complete Guide to Palmistry by Enid Huffman (1997)

Palmistry: The Whole View by Judith Hipskind (1998)

ADVANCED

The Art of Hand Analysis by Mir Bashir (1981) (if you can ignore the sexism)

Chinese Medical Palmistry by Xiao-Fab Zong and Gary Liscum (1995)

Destiny in the Palm of their Hand by Ghanshyam Singh Birla and David Frawley (2000)

Hand Book: Your Life is in Your Hands by Mark Seltman (2014)

Laws of Scientific Hand Reading by William G. Benham (1900)

Palmistry: The Language of the Hand by Cheiro (1894)

Traditional Chinese Hand and Foot Massage by Wu Genwei (2001)

ACKNOWLEDGMENTS

First, I want to offer thanks to my first palmistry teacher, Sushil Mukerjee, and to Arthur Remanjon, who gave me my first palmistry book that same year, which is still one of my favorites, *The Book of the Hand* by Fred Gettings. Thanks to Debbie Lewis, who sent me handprints for my collection for over a decade, and to all the strangers who have shared their hands and stories with me along the way. Blessings to Kristine Pidkameny and to the wonderful editors and illustrators at CICO Books for believing in my work and presenting it so beautifully.

I also want my wonderful friends who see those other dimensions with me to know how much I appreciate them, particularly Kate Greenway, Kate Levy, and Osla Thomason, and all those who support, challenge, and stretch me, including Terri Yellowhammer, Bridgette Cunningham, Virginia Allery, and Rachel and Wendell Held. Thanks to my inspiring astro-cohorts Alan Oken, Mark Woltz, and Anne Ortelee (another palmist of note), Arielle Guttman, and Frederick Woodruff. Gratitude goes to the communities that give me context: Twin Cities Reclaiming community, the crew at Eye of Horus, the Order of Bards, Ovates, and Druids, and Sharon Day and the Water Walkers. To Louise and Heid Erdrich, thank you for your inspiration of poetic authorship— it's an honor to know you. I send a big hug to my brother Steve Gottschalk and my grown children Max and Vanessa, whose hands and charts I watched from the minute they appeared, and who always give me honest feedback. Love to my patient, supportive mate, Dr Wren Walker Robbins—it's a joy to walk with you.